D1713618

MEMORIES UNLEASHED

Vietnam Legacy

CARL RUDOLPH SMALL

CASEMATE

Philadelphia & Oxford

Published in the United States of America and Great Britain in 2019 by
CASEMATE PUBLISHERS
1950 Lawrence Road, Havertown, PA 19083, USA
and
The Old Music Hall, 106–108 Cowley Road, Oxford OX4 1JE, UK

Copyright 2019 © Carl R. Small

Hardcover Edition: ISBN 978-1-61200-698-7
Digital Edition: ISBN 978-1-61200-699-4

A CIP record for this book is available from the British Library

Printed and bound in the United States of America

Typeset in India by Versatile PreMedia Services. www.versatilepremedia.com

For a complete list of Casemate titles, please contact:

CASEMATE PUBLISHERS (US)
Telephone (610) 853-9131
Fax (610) 853-9146
Email: casemate@casematepublishers.com
www.casematepublishers.com

CASEMATE PUBLISHERS (UK)
Telephone (01865) 241249
Email: casemate-uk@casematepublishers.co.uk
www.casematepublishers.co.uk

Dedication

I dedicate this book to Barbara, my wife. I refer to her in this book as Her; or, my Love. We met on a blind date. She, sixteen, still in high school: me, eighteen, graduated; working on bridge construction. Her father's words to her: "No daughter of mine is going to date a construction worker." He worked construction; a crane operator. She won him over.

She stood by me when I was at war, half a world away, putting her life on hold; not even attending her high school prom. She wrote every day: EVERY day. Her letters would bring my thoughts away for a moment from the hell of war; back to a quiet, gentle place: a place of peace; and love: we were married January 23rd, 1971, four months after I came home from Vietnam.

Throughout our journey together in life, we have had joyous moments: we bought a house; a small four-room ranch; not four bedrooms; four rooms total. It had a white picket fence out front: like the one we talked about on our dates as we sat in the car, sipping root beer floats in a frosted mug at the A & W drive-in diner. We worked together making it our home; remodeling it late at night; after we each finished our day jobs. Our parents called it building "sweat equity": it was really "sweat and tears equity". Our daughter, our only child, was born sixteen years after we were married; a miracle baby; a blessing. But there were also trying times; scary times: Barbs' first fight with cancer just a few years after we were married; winning it. Our daughter was eight when Barb fought cancer a second time: a different kind. As she fought it, she never slowed down being "mom"; wanting things to stay as normal as possible for our young daughter. She beat the cancer. Barb had her third fight with cancer about the time our first grandson was born, almost five years ago. During all the battles she fought with this enemy, she never mentioned the pain and discomfort; or fear: just saying to me "this is temporary; we will get through it": her words; that of a warrior. During her fights, the chemo slowly infused into her body, and engaged the enemy; the battle for life raged: the cancers were defeated because of her unshakable Faith in God; modern medicine; her tenacity for life; and uncompromising spirit.

She has awakened me from nightmares that I never wanted her to know. She never asked about them; just lay quietly with me, her hand touching me softly until I went back to sleep or downstairs for a hot chocolate. Her strength is her gentleness; she was the person I thought about after the missions; sometimes during them; reminding me of the good in the world.

I thank God for her: and I thank her, with all my heart, for making me a better man with her love.

Every word; tied to a thought:
Every thought; tied to an emotion:
Every emotion; tied to an experience:
Every experience; tied to a life:
Every life; tied to another.

Contents

Introduction

I joined the Marine Corps in 1969, nineteen years old, naïve, coming from Quechee, Vermont, a small farming community. After boot camp and specialty training, I landed in Da Nang, a PFC, assigned to 1/26/ Delta, a Marine Assault Force. I became part of a SLF (Special Landing Force). Our AO was I Corps; covering the area from the DMZ to below Da Nang; including the Islands and Marble Mountain. In late spring of 1970, that unit was pulled out of Vietnam. I was reassigned to 1/5/Alpha, another Marine Assault Force; AO still I Corps. Our work consisted of rapid response air-ground assaults to assist other assets that needed help. We were dropped in with choppers. Our missions ranged from company- or platoon-size search-and-destroy operations; to squad-sized day patrols and night actions (ambushes) and point element for mine sweepers. We were called upon for numerous security force actions such as for the Secretary of the Navy. We acted as first line of defense; positioned on the mountain pass surrounding Da Nang, for Bob Hope and other USO protections. Our unit worked with the ARVNs; the ROK (Republic of Korea) marines; the SOG (Special Operation Group); and Intel doing reconnaissance on enemy vills. We did pacification missions; working with CAP units to secure friendly vills from enemy forces. In the course of my thirteen-month tour of duty I rose up in rank to sergeant; youth and innocence lost.

The memories of Vietnam in this book are intertwined; some good; some bad. Some would wake me up at night as dreams, or nightmares. I started putting them down on little scraps of paper. I wasn't sure then, why, but felt drawn to doing it.

Four years after I came back from Vietnam, I was visiting my parents. During the course of the conversation, we went to look up some paperwork. I helped them sort through things. We came across old pictures and letters from Austria. My mother was Austrian. My dad had met there during World War II. Her and her family knew first-hand the cost of war. Her father and brother had been killed by the Nazis. Her family learned to hide by day and move at night. She toasted bread so it would last longer in her survival bag, living hand to mouth as they struggled to stay ahead of the Nazis. After the war, she married my dad and he brought her to America. She became a U.S. citizen. She always carried food in her purse. We thought it was to appease us; six hungry children; not knowing until years later of her fight for life in war.

I opened another drawer. A cardboard box, about the size a necklace would come in, fell to the floor. I picked it up and started to give it to my mother. She said it was dad's and opened it. It was a medal he was awarded from World War II. We knew he had fought in France and Germany and Austria. He had never talked about the war. I asked him why he had never said anything. His reply: "The same reason you don't talk about Vietnam." He closed the box and put it back in the drawer.

That moment became a memory. It is said that memories are pictures that the heart takes. I have used those words on occasion: at times when loved ones have moved away; or at funerals, hoping to console the bereaved left to deal with their shattered world. I believe those words to be true.

Forty-two years later, I had not spoken of this war, but had thought a lot about that day when I learned that such an important part of my father's legacy had not been known to us. Over the years after the war, I felt I never wanted my family to know what I had experienced. Realization came to me that I didn't want my family, or others, to miss that fragment of their history.

The Vietnam War became one of the most divisive wars in U.S. history. Subversive anti-U.S. government groups sprang up, unrest at colleges and universities turned from peaceful demonstrations to ugly, uncontrolled destruction and death.

People were bombarded daily with media-meted news of the war; only a finite group of people determined what the public saw or read about the real war. There was no Internet. No digital information could be relayed from a jungle firefight half a world away, to millions of people back home in an instant, allowing them to form an opinion based on raw data: unfiltered. The combat veteran, the true "boots on the ground," could tell them what the war was like; in real time; but few people wanted to listen.

The veterans of the Vietnam War came home; soul-tired; wounded in body or mind: or in a flag-draped coffin.... No other options. There were no ticker-tape parades; no keys to the city; no convoy of cars with flags flying, no crowds of people lining the streets cheering and running to touch their hand to meet them when they stepped off the bus. They were welcomed back to belittlement from some, shunned by others. Lucky ones, like me, came back to caring arms of family and loved ones, in a community that showed us thanks and honor, for fighting to help peace prevail.

Days or weeks after being home they looked for jobs for a person whose résumé included an honorable discharge. On the lines for past work experience it would read USMC-0311. That meant "Grunt"; ground-pounder; man-hunter. They'd had no time to build up a skill set of diverse technical experience: most had volunteered or had been drafted right after high school, some from college. The job search proved to be daunting, in some cases overwhelming. Most kept working hard to find hard work.

Memories Unleashed: Vietnam Legacy brings an exclusive perspective to the Vietnam veteran's story. People didn't understand what the veterans had been through. There are books and essays and articles written about the war. What makes *Memories Unleashed: Vietnam Legacy* unique and powerful is that it is written in such a way it brings you inside the marine; you see what he sees, feel what he feels. You know him; his back story; what he is thinking; why he made the decisions he needed to make.

I attended writing workshops and feedback for three years, writing *Memories Unleashed: Vietnam Legacy* for families, including my own, to know what their loved ones had been through. There are no names mentioned in its entirety. I wrote it to be a message to all veteran families to show the price the veteran paid for freedom. The chapters were written individually, at different times. It was only when I put the pieces together that revealed it was also a love story. A story of people pulled apart by war; some never to see the other again. The war had impacted them all.

CHAPTER I

Goodbye; For a Year or Forever

The marine slid his sea bag closer to the door that led to the tarmac. Not just a sea bag any longer; now his war bag. His tailored khaki uniform formed to his lean, muscular frame. The crease of his shirt sleeve pressed perfectly through the center of his P.F.C. rank chevron. Sunlight shone through the window onto his young face. It was the only window in the airport terminal. The room, about the length of two picnic tables, had one entry door from the parking lot; one desk for information, ticket sales and baggage labeling. A sign nailed to the wall above the only other door read "exit to terminal, bring your luggage". The room: full of his loved ones. A plane's propellers vibrated the glass window. He looked up to the top of the control tower, next to the runway. The tower, three stories high; had only room for two people; one on duty. This was a small airport, running an air-shuttle service to the closest major transportation hub, 150 miles away.

His mother and father and siblings, his girlfriend and her parents all had their private thoughts they told to him. The mother was saying goodbye. She spoke with a heavy German accent, having come from Austria. She had met the father in that war. She hugged her son, hard, not wanting to let him go, tears running down her cheeks. She had lost her father and brother in the other war.

"Don't get hurt. God keep you safe," she said, her final words. This was her first son to go to this war.

They'd had a quiet talk earlier. It was one of those rare moments when a mother of six kids gets to talk alone with one. He had completed boot camp and then graduated from four weeks specialized individual combat training. Only a few days left of a two-week leave. They knew now where his orders would send him. Eleven-thirty in the morning; he came into the kitchen for a drink. She slid the blackened kettle to the front of the stove, hands shaking. He grabbed one of her hot homemade biscuits, twisting off the top. It opened into his hand. He brought it up to his mouth. The warm scent of home forever locked in.

He put his arm around her shoulders, grabbed the teapot, and turned her, as in the Viennese waltz she had taught him, to the old white cast sink with the wooden two-by-four replacement legs. They put the kettle under the spout of the kitchen faucet. She started laughing as they filled the kettle together.

"Everything will be alright. I won't get hurt." He said to her. "I'll need a cup of tea and a hot biscuit when I get back home."

The father had been in the Army around ten years, taking a break in the middle, rejoining for World War II, the last four years in combat liberating Europe. He knew the price it retracts from a person, the price the family would pay waiting and praying for his safe return. They had talked alone earlier; about life and war and death; matter of factly; laying emotion aside.

"Don't ever get wounded…" his father had said, looking straight into his eyes. "Don't ever get hurt…" he said again. The son knew what he meant. Any letters to them would be good letters. Then his father, who had not hugged him since grade school, put his arms around him, holding for a short while before letting him go. All in private; in the crowd, he shook his hand and wished him luck.

His girlfriend's family had two sons of their own in the service, knowing what it meant to wait for their safe return; they were saying goodbye again to a loved one.

"Stay low and come back home," her father said and held his handshake a little longer.

"You will always be in our prayers. Don't get hurt and come back safe," her mother said and hugged him. Sometimes she had made them toasted tuna sandwiches when he was there late at night.

"Don't forget. I'll want another toasted tuna when I get back," he said with a smile.

The hardest to say goodbye to: his girlfriend; his Love. They knew they would be married when he returned. He physically ached saying goodbye, the rapid beat of his heart, his chest nearing explosion. The first night he saw her, they were going on a blind date as a favor to their friends, the first blind date either had gone on; a double date with another couple. He watched her in the rear view mirror as she walked to his car, with her friend, under the streetlight.

Slacks hugged her petite shape. Shoulder-length brunette hair bounced as she walked. Her hands were thrust into her back pockets, hips swaying sensually. A chocolate-colored suede jacket, zipped up, molded to the form of her breasts. Reaching over the four-on-the-floor shift, he opened the door, the dome light coming on. She slid onto the front seat, looking at him with her dark brown eyes and a smile that lit up her face.

The Marine with his Love before he went to war.

"Thank You God" he murmured, stunned by her beauty, then blushed, hoping no one heard, as he had meant it to be a silent thought.

He told her first where he was headed, but not until the last part of his two-week leave. She had surmised it. Where else did they send marines but to war? She had cried hard: "body-shaking" hard: "gasping for air" hard: "tears never stopping" hard. They held each other, an eternal embrace.

His spoken promise to her: "I won't get hurt. I'll be back and we'll spend the rest of our lives together."

He held her last before boarding the plane. Her soft lips pressed hard against his. Their fierce embrace pressing each body into the other. A memory meant to last a year or forever, the final memory before stepping on; to war.

25,000 Mornings

The number of days in an average lifetime is 25,000. This day was his day number 7,340. The alarm went off at 0100. Anticipation had made sleep impossible, stirring his blood. The bare bottoms of his feet felt the smooth tile of the shower room, the steaming hot water pelting his lean body.

"How long will it be before I feel tile under my feet and hot water again." The bar of soap broke in his hand, crushed against his stomach. Bringing the pieces to his face, he inhaled the clean scent. The mirror above the sink reflected the image of the man deep in thought, eyes closed as if in prayer, before the shower's mist encompassed them as in a morning fog.

Pressed khakis bloused near the top of his black, spit-shined boots; the ironed green shirt with the rank insignia creased down the exact center; the Eagle, Globe and Anchor pinned on the front left side of his soft-cover completed his preparation. He picked up his sea bag and walked out of the marine barracks, headed to his ride to the tarmac. The darkness of the California morning shielded the mass movement going on at the base.

Their plane lifted off into the darkness, the thrust of the rapid take-off pushing him back into his seat. He looked out the window, his heart hurting like an open wound as he watched the lights of his homeland become smaller and smaller, turning into a distant tiny star just before disappearing into the blackness. Destination: Vietnam.

They made a quick stop and plane change in Hawaii, shuffled from one plane to the other, walking the corridor between concertina wires strung out on both sides of them, like criminals. That was hours ago. The plane started to descend. All eyes focused out the windows. Boyish faces on grown men pressed against the glass looked down at the land that unfolded beneath, a picture just coming into focus.

The mountains reminded him of the green mountains of Vermont. They were a darker green; the deep green of the vine-end of a watermelon in July. The jungle canopy was thick and unrevealing of its secrets underneath. Foothills sloped into valleys. Straw-thatched huts of the villages dotted the centers. Rice paddies surrounded them, water glistening; their earthen borders lay out in blocks.

Their plane lined up with the distant runway, the vehicles on the airstrip resembling ants moving on a parking lot. The plane touched down, stirring up the red dust of Da Nang. Silence came over the men on board. Some faces blank, curiosity in others. All knew from this moment their lives would be changed forever.

Outside the hatched door, the heat struck him. Not the temperature, though it was over one hundred degrees; the heat of activity. People were moving everywhere; running or a fast walk. Planes with their cargo doors open being loaded with stacks of equipment on fork lifts driving into the belly of these the beasts; swallowed whole. F-4 Phantom jets were taking off, the thunderous roar deafening. Their bombs and rockets would be death for some; life for others.

He stopped at the last step of the plane's ramp, pointing to groups of men carrying long black bags into the belly of another plane.

"What are they loading?" he asked the corporal meeting him.

"Body bags…"

A chopper flew him and two other marines to their new platoon. He had met them on the plane; they had exchanged names and home-towns; made a pact to keep in touch with each other when they found out who they would be assigned to. They arrived at a sandbagged bunkered fire base. Between somewhere and nowhere he thought. Orientation, clothing, armament, squad placement; they assigned him to 2nd Squad; the others went to 1st Squad. Introductions to his squad were quick. They were preparing for their night patrol in the Zone.

"Saddle up," his squad leader ordered. His squad moved out. "Lock and Load." He slid in a clip, drew back the bolt, and released it; SHIICCKK... The sound of the bullet being chambered. Darkness had fallen on Day 7,340.

Inauguration to War: Day One

The quietness was loud. Cold beads of sweat rolled down his forehead. No one talked; they used hand motions, to break the unity with the night could bring swift retribution. The young marine's placement in his squad: in the middle; just behind the squad leader; his protection from the night. The footsteps sloshing in the rice paddy stirred up a damp, musty smell of garden plants.

The hand of his squad leader motioned down, with urgent movements. Blood rushed through his body; a body acting on its own, not waiting for options for the mind to choose. He felt, rather than saw, his team drop to the ground. His breathing was rapid yet it seemed stopped.

Figures in the night walked in tight single file down the berm of the adjacent paddy dike, thirty-five to forty yards away. They were taller than he had imagined them. They seemed almost carefree. The rifles they carried betrayed the lie. They were in the kill-zone.

The illumination round flashed up into the sky a split second before he heard the bark of a rifle open fire. All around him he saw the muzzle flashes, heard the sounds of firepower from the M-60 machine gun, the gunner screaming directions to the ammo man, the urgent voice of the squad leader directing their fire. He yanked his clip out and spun it over, slamming home the one he had taped to the bottom. He didn't have to hear the click of an empty chamber. He subconsciously had counted the eighteen rounds gone from his first clip. The bullets hit their mark. They fell, some still moving, some not. Fifteen rounds gone, three left. He reached for another clip from his bandolier; seventeen rounds gone, one left.

Screams filled the air, louder it seemed, than the crushing sound of the fresh clip slammed home. Four rounds gone, fourteen left. The illumination round just popped after streaking into the sky in a timeless arch, its brilliance lighting up the zone as it floated down in its tiny parachute. He heard the distinctive crack of the AK. Warm, sticky liquid ran down the inside of his right forearm. Eleven rounds gone, seven left. No return fire. No sight of them, even with the strong light of the illumination round still floating from the sky. The strong, arid smell of gun-powder lingered. The moaning sounds of the hurt drifted across the rice paddy.

Casualty count: his squad all okay. No need to mention the flesh wound. He had wrapped his bandana around it and rolled down his sleeve. There was more to do. It was his first night in-country and he still had a year or forever to go.

The Names

The terror of the firefight: the euphoria of survival. The emotions of the young marine surged as he stared into the trees at the rice paddy's edge. His eyes strained in the darkness watching for more of the enemy. He knelt on one knee, his rifle raised, ready for another assault. The adrenaline pulsed through his body. "Are there more here?" he whispered.

"Pray we don't find out," the squad's point man answered: his voice calm; the words chilling.

The firefight over, the enemy down, his squad leader had deployed the three-man fire team that included the young marine, to the tree line to secure that direction from another assault. The three-man machine-gun team guarded their flank. The remaining six marines checked the enemy causalities. He saw the enemy figures lying motionless in the rice paddy as he ran beyond them toward the tree line: death within arm's reach; death he'd abetted to; yet darkness hid its faces.

He heard the choppers coming and looked up. Two Cobra gunship choppers skimmed the tree line, protecting the three transport choppers that they escorted. His squad leader ordered a defensive perimeter around the site and popped a flare. The transport choppers landed; the Cobras flew just above, ready to fire down on any enemy. The choppers with the casualties now aboard lifted back up into the night.

He heard rifle fire break out to the east; another firefight. He counted the seconds between seeing the muzzle flashes before the sound reached them; four, maybe five seconds: over a mile away: 1st Squad's operation area. They had left the base twenty minutes before them. Lumination flares burst in the distance. The realization of war surrounded him: a shudder went through his body.

His squad leader assembled the squad. "Everybody, get focused. We're moving to our alternate site. Point man, move out." The night was not half over; seven hours till daylight.

They returned to base as dawn broke. The silence echoed. The young marine sat on his cot, motionless: His breathing slow and deep. He gripped his rifle and stared at his hands. His squad's voices outside the canvas wall seemed distant, inaudible. Words floated by: firefight; gooks; new guy. His inauguration to war: His first night in-country: his first firefight. He survived.

He took a deep breath, pursed his lips and exhaled slow; his nerves taut. They were told that 1st Squad were ambushed by VC; the squad wiped out; all twelve marines KIA. He didn't know 1st Squad: except for two; the two that he talked with on the plane coming here. He saw their faces. He laughed with them. He stared out the plane's window with them. They saw the land of war together as they came into Da Nang. They deplaned right behind him. He flew with them on the chopper that brought them to the platoon. He was assigned to 2nd Squad; they were assigned to 1st Squad.

"See ya around," he had said to them.

"You bet," they'd said to him.

That was yesterday.

He tried to think of their names. He wrote them down on a piece of paper he'd ripped out of a magazine on the plane. He got up from his cot and went to his backpack. He took out his notebook. He couldn't find the slip of paper: their names were gone.

He yelled out loud. He tore the pages from his book, ripped them into pieces and threw them across the hooch. He grabbed his towel from his neck and rubbed at the blood and the mud on his rifle. His squad leader burst into the hooch. Shredded paper flew into the air. "You okay?" he was asked.

"Just cleaning up," he answered.

"It's always going to be hard. Sometimes not everybody comes back," his squad leader said. Get some rest. We go out again in four hours."

CHAPTER 2

Mortars and Miracles

The marine's squad entered the forward command base's field of fire. The point man pulled the pin on a smoke grenade and threw it off to their left flank. The loud pop as the grenade burst broke the stillness. Red smoke spewed out, signaling the squad's return from their day patrol. They passed through the concertina wire and sandbagged bunkers, raw nerves starting to relax, entering the inner sanctum of the base. He said a silent prayer of thanks that their patrol had gone well. It had been a week since they had made contact with the enemy in that abandoned vill. Maybe the VC had enough. But he couldn't shake his apprehension.

"Get some shut-eye," his squad leader said, passing inside the last perimeter bunker. He got to their hooch; dropped his helmet, five bandoliers of ammo (six hundred thirty rounds), two canteens (now empty), one claymore, his poncho; and flak jacket with four grenades, seven salt tablets, and one melted piece of homemade fudge he was saving—from her—wrapped in tinfoil in the pockets. He was relieved of all their weight; but still harnessed to the weight of war. He kept his green towel draped around the back of his neck, his M-16 with his taped double clip in his right hand.

He rolled out his poncho and lay down, his flak jacket as his pillow, laying his rifle next to him, his left arm through the rope sling. Darkness would soon engulf them. He heard the 1st Squad saddling up for their night patrol. They were marines brought in to form the new 1st Squad; the others had been KIA. Tiredness ached through his body. His gut wanted something to eat. But he was torn. Sleep won out over eating.

He dreamed of his Love. They were waltzing to their song "Someday We'll Be Together." Her hands were clasped behind his neck; his hands caressed her lower back. Her hair brushed his face. He drew in the scent of her; the Wind Song perfume; both bound within his soul. Their bodies pressed together, moving as one. Before the night erupted into Hell, he was in Heaven.

The explosion jarred him awake. He jumped, rifle in his hand, finger on the trigger lock. He threw on his flak jacket and helmet, grabbed his ammo, and ran towards the sandbagged perimeter line. The incoming mortar whistled towards its target, the blast shook his world.

He tried to get up and couldn't.

He tried to see, or hear, but couldn't.

Absolute quiet and darkness… He waited for God.

A warm wetness trickled from his ears. His face pressed against the ground, the pungent red dirt in his mouth and nose, the strong smell of gunpowder lingering in the air. Feeling the weight of the earth covering him, feeling his rifle in his right hand, he sorted his scrambled brain, not sure what had happened. If I were dead, would I be able to feel?

The dirt on top of him shifted as he struggled to get up. He was in a shallow hole. An illumination round bursting above him lit up the assault on the base. Sounds were muffled like they were at a great distance away.

Rifle fire: M-60 fire: claymores blasting: voices yelling. He crawled out and staggered the twenty yards to the perimeter, like a moth drawn to light, falling against another marine.

"Your ears are bleeding. Corpsman up!" the marine at the perimeter wall yelled.

"Don't get them. I'll be okay," he said, wiping the blood with his towel. The noise still seemed distant and muted even though he knew it was right next to him.

The full assault never came. The VC attack was limited, a few mortars and AK fire. They never showed themselves. His ears had stopped bleeding. His balance was still shaky. He walked back to get his canteen to wash his face, and passed the hole he had fallen in. Two mortars had landed close to each other. The first one woke him up, making him run to the line. In the darkness, the crater invisible, he had fallen into it just as the second shell hit. The enemy's first mortar had shielded him from most of the blast from the second.

Miracles happen, even in war. His promise to her: I won't get hurt.

CHAPTER 3

Don't Go to Heaven Alone

The marine scraped a foxhole in the ground, his Ka–Bar knife and his hands the only tools. He made it just big enough for him to sit and to turn in. He didn't know when the enemy would come, only that they would. The rest of the marine's platoon was making their foxholes in the mountainside, fifteen to twenty feet apart. The sulfur-like stench of the napalm from the air strike on the enemy still lingered. It took his breath, burned his eyes; one of the most horrific weapons known to man.

Small areas on the strike zone still had an orange glow. He tried to forget the bodies. He had picked a mountain orchid on the way up the mountain earlier. He took it out from his pocket, and drew in its sweet scent, cleansing out the putrid odor of the napalm before putting it back. The silence of the night sent a chill down his body. The NVA would be back.

He finished his foxhole and sheathed his Ka–Bar, then checked his rifle and ammo.

"I'm putting out the claymores," he said to the marines on each side, taking two claymores down the hill. A branch snapped. He stared into the darkness, eyes focused toward the sound: nothing. Then a noise came again. A different sound: like dragging a sack of grain across a wooded pasture. He moved his rifle up in front of his body, keeping his profile unbroken and thumbed the button to full auto. He heard a gasp. Training told him to fire, a silent whisper told him to wait.

The gasp came again. A shadow jerked up the hill toward him. It got closer; a man trying to crawl to him; no weapon; naked. The stink of napalm hit him hard. The man had been in the napalm attack. His clothes were burned off; legs gone from the knees down, as was his left arm below the bicep; only his thumb and forefinger remained on his right hand; most of his lower face was gone.

The napalm had done one last horrific thing. It seared his blood vessels. His skin still burned; an unbelievable painful death. He reached up to the marine, and handed him a tiny piece of thick paper. The marine took it, and reached down to pick him up. The man shook his head. He pointed to the scrap of paper, then to himself, and scratched a hole in ground, motioned putting them in and covered it back in. He wanted to be buried with the paper. The marine nodded.

He wasn't sure of the man's religion. He assumed NVA, maybe a villager passing through, or a prisoner, caught in the napalm hell. The man held his finger to his own head with his thumb straight up. He wanted to be shot, his pain so great. The marine could not.

He knelt down next to the man and put down his rifle, wrapped his arms around the man's shoulders, gently pulling him to his chest. Death was coming for him; soon. He started to whisper sing into the man's ear a children's Bible song. He didn't know why, it just came out.

"Jesus loves you, this we know; for the Bible tells us so," gently rocking him. The man looked up at him; then beyond. His body relaxed, then slumped lifeless against the marine.

He carried him up the hill, laying him next to his foxhole, and then took out his pen light in the bottom of the foxhole, shielded by his poncho. The piece of paper was part of a black and white photograph; only the very righthand side and bottom was there, the rest burned away. It showed part of a woman's head, no face, from the ear over and just long hair that fell almost to her waist. The bottom showed two pairs of feet, one pair slender, and the other larger. The man wanted to be buried with her; a last request. He started digging his foxhole longer.

"Afraid they'll see ya?" the marine next to him asked, not seeing he had carried something back.

"Only God knows," he answered, and kept digging. Finished, he pulled the body in, laid the picture next to the man's heart, and put the man's hand over it. They would hold hands for eternity. He took his towel from around his neck and wiped the dirt from the body then gently laid the towel over the man's face and chest, covering the picture, and pulled the loose dirt over him, pressing it down quietly.

He reached into his flack-jacket pocket and took out the mountain orchid he picked on the way up the mountain. Its sweet scent of serenity created an aura of peace. The marine laid it on the grave. God had this all planned he thought. He started to pray;

"Our Father who art in Heaven…" He heard the noise in front of them; NVA.

His church confirmation flashed through his mind.

"Don't go to Heaven alone, take someone with you," the priest had said. He had meant conversion.

The marine thought of the priest's words and the Vietnamese man he had just sang to and prayed over. He leveled his rifle towards the enemy. Tonight, the priest's words could have a dual meaning.

Point of No Return

He guided the marine squad through the night in the kill zone, his new meat label gone. He had proven his skill in the bush. Mosquitoes swarmed around him; feasting in his ears, on his face; his lips swollen from their attacks. He was afraid to swat them for fear of being detected. His heart beat rapid in his chest. He swallowed hard, gulping in air. "Yea, though I walk through the valley of the shadow of death, I shall fear no evil," he whispered in prayer. Nerves pushed to the edge of breakdown. His legs felt weighted. He searched for silhouettes that moved or anything that didn't fit in; stopping and listening, all senses straining for signs of the enemy. This was his first night as point man. He had been in-country for less than a month.

The marine sponged sweat from his face with his towel. Something lay next to the pagoda ahead. The hair stood up on the back of his neck. He dropped to one knee, sending a silent warning to the squad.

He could not see beyond the pagoda, thirty feet away; the length of a short country driveway. The figure had not moved. His squad leader made his way up and knelt next to him. They needed to know if they were walking into an ambush; if the figure was alone. The point man slung his rifle around to his back and pulled his Ka-Bar from its sheath.

"Are you okay with this?" whispered his squad leader.

"It's mine to do," he replied.

He crawled toward his target; silence his armor, muscles taut. The darkness played tricks on his sight. It looked like the enemy was moving, then not. He tightened his grip on the knife as he came up behind the figure. Fear pumped adrenaline through his veins, force feeding his nerves. His mind demanded; would the darkness shut off from God's sight what he was about to do to? He posed to strike; the decision made; the target his.

The target repositioned, uttering a grunt noise. The point man stared in disbelief as the target dug its hooves into the ground, making an indent to get comfortable.

It was a sleeping wild pig.

He backed away, his hands shook, never relieving the stress of an action not taken. He put his Ka-Bar back in its sheath and crawled back to his squad. He hid his fear. Not the fear of walking point; but of passing a moral point of no return.

The Bumblebee

The point man's leg muscles knotted from limping. His blisters oozed, rubbed raw by his water-soaked stateside boots. The leather stayed wet;

his feet never dried. Almost sixty days in-country and still no jungle boots for him in company supply.

Rain came last night as they laid on the ground in their ambush site and watched for enemy movement; pounding rain; soaking rain; mercifully stopping as dawn broke; the start of the monsoon season. Soon the rain won't stop for weeks. Today the hot sun would have everything baked dry by ten hundred hours; except for his feet.

He led the twelve-man squad up the valley. A one-man scout chopper flew ahead of the marine squad. It was the size of a pup tent with rotor blades and two rail landing skies. The buzzing of its engine sounded like a bumblebee as it broke the silent advance of their search-and-destroy mission. It darted in un-patterned zig-zags a few feet off the ground, just a stone's throw ahead of him. The chopper spun in sudden rotation, the pilot now facing the point man. He smiled, waved in a saluting gesture. The point man couldn't help but to smile and flashed the "V" for peace back at him. The chopper lifted straight up into the air, treetop height, leveled off and darted across the top of the trees that were ahead of them, the length of two football fields.

The point man had never worked with a Bumblebee scout chopper. He marveled at the degree of proficiency the pilot flew; as if he was a puff of wind controlled by nature, blowing along the horizon. The pilot's job; scout ahead of the marine patrol and draw enemy fire. The marines', job destroy the enemy when they fired on the bumblebee. His squad leader signaled for a halt and came up to him.

"The lieutenant wants to let the scout bird get further ahead." he said. "How are your feet?" he asked.

"If it gets too far, we won't be able to cover him as good. I think the pilot is crazy or has a death wish." the point man said. He didn't answer the feet question.

"Why do you think he's crazy?" his squad leader asked.

"He's flying out front to find enemy or draw fire." the point man said.

"We're his guardians. We make sure nothing happens to him from our end. You're doing the same thing he is, except you're on the ground." his squad leader said, his face solemn. "The difference is, he can fly the hell out of the way. We can't. The only way clear for us is to stop the enemy."

The squad moved out through the trees. Their mission was winding down; a one week op around the base of Charlie Ridge. Their mission was to search out any VC encampments and destroy ammo or food supplies stockpiled for the monsoon season. They were headed for their extraction point. ETA 1430; three hours away.

"God help my feet," he whispered, not sure he could take the pain much longer.

Another hour passed when his squad was stopped by the lieutenant's orders.

"We will stop here for a while. We've got heavy rain coming in soon. Command base is working to extract us before it starts," his squad leader said.

The point man heard the Bumblebee scout fly over. He looked up. The chopper was high, right above him, circling slowly; their look-out from the sky.

The point man started to choke with emotion. He wasn't sure if it was the pain in his feet; or the sudden realization that the bond of brotherhood of each watching out for the other was unbreakable. He took off his boots; his feet now a pussy mass. He reached into his pack, pulled out a plastic bag; in it a pair of dry socks. He wrung out his wet ones, using them to wipe over the open sores. He looked quickly around, hopping no-one had seen; not wanting special treatment. He put the fresh socks on, wincing in pain as he slid his boots back on. Jungle issue boots would have been dry. "God, please get us home before rain. I don't know how much further I can go." he prayed in a quiet whisper. His lieutenant had put in requisitions for jungle boots but the resupply of his size never seemed to get to him. They were always gone whenever they came back in from an op.

"Extraction choppers here in twenty minutes, set up defensive perimeter for LZ." said their squad leader.

The point man waited anxiously as he scanned the tree line and hills for enemy movement. This was the time the enemy would choose to hit the squad; when the choppers came in to lift them out; the choppers a prime target. He heard the loud hum of the Bumblebee scout chopper, He saw him rapidly flying in a circle above them watching, working to cover the area around them for any enemy. The point man felt the rush of adrenalin flow through his body as the dark specks flying up the valley grew larger; their extraction chopper with two gunship escorts. The Bumblebee made one low pass over the squad and shot up over the trees. In just seconds he was out of sight in the clouds that were closing in rapidly.

"God keep him safe," the point man whispered, knowing he had stayed longer then he should have to watch over them.

The rain poured down on them as the squad walked from the command base LZ. The downpour had commenced as they started their flight back down the valley. The choppers had got there just in time to get them out. The point man walked into the squad's hooch and sat on his cot. He took off his boots and wrapped his feet in a towel. He started wiping his rifle down when he heard someone come in.

"Hey point man, got something for ya." his squad leader said. It was a pair of jungle boots, size eleven; his size. "Fresh from supply: your name's on the tag. It seems a certain bird colonel flying in a Bumblebee saw you having trouble with your feet. He got word to the lieutenant who filled him in on the supply trouble. These came for you about an hour ago."

CHAPTER 4

Underwater Terror

The three-man marine point team broke through the tall jungle grass and stopped at the river's edge. The rest of the squad waited a hundred yards behind them in the jungle. The sight before the Leader was like a peacock's tail. Brown water wound around the dark green jungle island, the blue afternoon sky inset as nature's backdrop. The leader looked across the intimidating flow. They had to cross to the island and clear it of the enemy.

They started into the warm, leech-filled water: fear not an option for not checking out the island. He reached mid-stream, the depth about chest high. His next step found no bottom. He plunged under. He held his rifle high above his head. His feet landed on the bottom and he thrust himself upward. When his face broke above the surface, he saw that his teammates were neck deep and still walking. He gasped for a breath, and felt the warm muck close over his head as he went back under. He prayed the bottom would be closer. He hit and bounced back to the surface. He heard laughter as his team joked about being taller than he. "Keep watching the island, you shit-birds," he yelled, and then went under again. His mouth still open, he swallowed the vile water.

They struggled out of the water on the shore of the island and started their sweep through the steamy jungle vegetation. They worked their way across the tiny island, spread out but within sight of each other. They could cover it quicker. Near the back side the leader heard the screams of one of his team. He swung toward the scream, his rifle ready to target the enemy. His teammate ran backwards; eyes focused on the ground; wild with fear. A brown snake, thick as his arm and as long as a garden hoe chased him. The snake held his head a foot off the ground. His tongue flickered. The snake saw the other marine and slithered away deeper into the jungle island. "Payback," he told his team mate. The leader laughed this time. They swept the island, determined it all clear, except for snakes. He singled his team and they entered the river again to cross back over and rejoin their squad.

He led them out of the river then raised his hand to stop. He looked north; the direction his squad should be. He saw jungle; no marines. He swallowed hard. The squad had the radio. He must make visual contact to hook up with them. He moved his men up the river's edge; all eyes toward the jungle. They came to a bend in the river. He did not want to go much further without knowing exactly where they were. He scanned the vegetation. He saw the squad leader's hand raised high; motioning him to them. Relief flashed through his body. The squad would move as one unit to higher ground, away from rivers and snakes when darkness set in, toward the enemy that waited ahead.

CHAPTER 5

Road of Trouble

The point man led the squad forward. They were the buffer between any enemy in the tree line and the dirt highway, fifty yards to the right. VC had planted mines in the road during the night. Three VC had been stopped, two disappeared into the darkness. The road had to be checked out. The explosives engineers moved up the highway sweeping their mine detectors back and forth over the road. The supply convoys and civilians on the road were held back. Villagers watched from the open area next to the tree line. Their gardens and vills were just on the

other side of it. The Cobra gunships flew above the treetops, next to the road, ready to unleash a firestorm down on any VC; a deadly place for the villagers to be.

He looked back to the road. He saw a marine convoy that waited to move on.

"Lord, keep them safe," the point man whispered. His Love's brother drove in a convoy.

It was early morning; still cool. He looked to the tree line for any sign of movement; the squad a prime target for ambush; no cover for them. His steel helmet strapped tight on his head replaced his bush hat. He had stuffed that between his middle back and belt, it was now soaked from the cold sweat of fear that rolled down his back. His flak jacket, never before snapped in front, now snapped tight up to his neck. No movement in the tree line. He scanned the ground for fresh-turned dirt, or a glint of wire, or any type of armament that was cast aside; anything that was different: all signs of booby traps. They had started out two hours ago at dawn. He was getting mentally impatient. I need to move faster he thought. No! Go slow, damn it. If anything is missed, there would be no second chance.

For two more hours the point man led the squad. The sun close to midway across the sky, the heat and humidity took its toll. He was drenched; sweat flowing from his body. He had noticed the villagers had moved back beyond the tree line. He breathed a sigh of relief; that much less to be worried about.

He didn't know how far they had come since morning or how far they would be escorting the mine-sweep. He heard the mine-sweep team yell out. They had stopped. The squad leader ordered a stop. The squad dropped to one knee and faced the tree line, ready for an ambush. An engineer came to the edge of the road to talk to the squad leader.

"Another sweep team has checked the road ahead. You will be cleared to leave. We're headed back," he said.

"Take a break," the squad leader said, turning to the squad.

The point man sat next to the road and unsnapped his flak jacket. He poured water into his hand and washed the sweat from his face. The convoy was moving past. He watched the drivers go by; a chance to see his Love's brother. The trucks began to gain speed, the roar of their

engines louder as the drivers geared up their speed. Not because of an interrupted schedule: it was harder to hit a moving target. The point man doubted he would recognize his Love's brother anyway, having only met him once back home. But the roar of the trucks made him feel good. If this was her brother's convoy, he had helped keep him safe.

CHAPTER 6

The Crucifix and the Crossroads

The point man crawled back to his squad. The moon was young and cast shadows on the side of the mountain they called Charlie Ridge: a VC haven and travel route to the vills: a kill zone. He had set out the two claymore mines facing the VC trail. His hand cupped the detonation wires. He moved back; letting them slide through his fingers; checking for breaks in the wire or anything that could be wrong. The claymore blast would inflict damage to the enemy; and confusion. The element of surprise would give the twelve-man marine squad the crucial first five seconds of the ambush.

He moved to where the squad was set in. He laid the wires with their triggers next to his rifle. He went through his mental checklist; field of vision, position of squad, ammo, grenades; all okay. He pulled his green towel over his head to fend off the mosquitoes, but left a hole to see through. He started to whisper his private prayer and reached for his crucifix around his neck. It wasn't there. He reached down his flak jacket. No neck chain; no crucifix. He felt around the ground: gone: lost on the way to the site or out by the claymores. Deep sorrow swept over him: the crucifix given to him by his Love's mother. He whispered his private prayer.

"And help me find the crucifix," he added.

The squad watched the trail and waited. The moon grew older. The point man laid his head close to the ground and brought his canteen to his lips. He pulled his sleeve up past his watch and cupped his hand around it. The Timex's luminous hands showed ten minutes after midnight.

He let his sleeve back down and looked back at the trail. He held his breath to listen better; a sound caught his focus. He saw movement on the trail. He reached over and touched the squad leader, the signal that enemy was here. His fingers curled around the claymores' triggers; one in each hand. He stared at the trail. The movement had stopped. He saw nothing. The squad waited. Adrenaline flushed through his body; taut nerves begged to be released; the rapid beat of his heart the only sound. No images floated down the trail. Maybe he had stared too long. Trees would walk if you stared hard enough. Maybe his mind created the figures; maybe.

The trail itself started to move. The enemy a part of it; bushes stuck into their clothes to blend with it.

His squad leader opened fire, springing the ambush. The point man squeezed the triggers on both claymores. Man-made lightning flashed on the trail when they exploded; the blasts thundered down the ridge; the marines fired into the enemy.

One thousand one:

The machine gun sprayed the enemy; screams came from the trail; sounds of pain; fear; confusion.

One thousand two:

The point man dropped the claymore triggers, grabbed his rifle, and fired at the figures he couldn't see two seconds ago. The marine squad had fire superiority, never letting up the onslaught of firepower onto the enemy. No return fire yet.

One thousand three:

The point man's clip was close to empty; his left hand ready with another clip. He heard the marine squad's automatic rifleman change clips.

One thousand four:

Figures from the tail end of the VC column were trying to run back up the mountain. The squad leader directed the machine-gun fire to the upper end of the trail. The point man fired the last three rounds in his clip; thumbed the eject button, the empty clip dropped out. He slammed the fresh clip in. The VC returned fire, the distinctive sound of their AK rifles mingled into the mayhem of the firefight. Muzzle flashes from a VC's rifle pointed up to the marine position. The ground in front of the point man caught a VC's bullet. Dirt flew into his face. He emptied his clip at the muzzle flashes: the muzzle flashes stopped.

One thousand five:

The enemy force was broken up; the first eight or ten VC had taken the full force of the claymores. They were not moving; or not able to return fire; other of the enemy confused; not yet knowing where the marines were; still others just froze in fear. The marines' blitz overwhelmed the enemy.

The squad leader called command base for illumination on their position, and for a fire mission for mortars toward the north where the VC had run back up the mountain.

In ten minutes: hell was over; no return fire from the VC. The marines advanced toward the trail and swept the area. Most of the enemy dead: three wounded prisoners. The marines retrieved AKs and RPGs, and a plastic-lined cloth bag with papers and maps. Mortars pounded the upper trail for another thirty minutes.

Three intel choppers with ARVN interpreters flew in after the firefight. One of the choppers lifted off right after they landed, taking the three prisoners and the papers and maps in the plastic-lined bag. The enemy bodies and their armament were loaded into the other two.

"You guys stopped an enemy courier element," the interpreter said. The squad secured the site till daylight.

Morning light lifted the veil of darkness. The point man led the squad out on the leader's command. He made the sign of the cross as he walked up the trail.

"Lord, be with us," he prayed. They went up the ridge to check for any VC that had escaped the ambush or the mortar fire. He wished they could travel back the original trail. He wanted to look for the crucifix. He knew they could not. Half a mile up the ridge they turned and came down a different path. The sun was midway of the sky when he stopped at a crossroads. It was part of the trail they had come in on. He wiped the sweat from his face with his green towel, and looked down the old trail. Fifteen yards ahead the trail started to turn. He saw the sun reflect off metal; his crucifix.

He dropped to the ground, off to the side of the trail; the squad behind him fell to the same side; ready for ambush. He thumbed the button of his rifle to full auto. Crawling closer; watching both sides of the trail, he went half the distance; no enemy to be seen. But he remembered last night; the bushes in their clothes. He lay still. Five minutes: no movement. Ten minutes: still no movement: he crept closer. Five yards from the glimmer: no enemy. A cautious smile came to his face. His crucifix's chain caught on a bush. He moved closer; slow: it could still be an ambush. He lay quiet, and looked into the brush all around: nothing. He reached up for the crucifix: it fell into his hand.

CHAPTER 7

Precious Seconds—Precious Life

The midnight darkness cloaked the nine-man marine squad: three men short; their machine-gun team. They crossed the valley floor, a main travel route for the enemy; a kill zone. The point man led them through fields of knee-high grass and past narrow bands of trees crisscrossing at random. The land itself fought him. Man-high elephant grass with razor-edged leaves that sliced into flesh confronted him now. No short way around. He didn't know how far it went. He stopped and peered into the thick stalks of grass. He rolled down his sleeves, glancing back at the squad as he wiped the sweat from his face. He tucked his towel tight around his neck.

He checked his compass bearings. He could not see the valley wall on the other side, the night too black; the grass too high; like going through a corn maze on Halloween night. He led the squad into the elephant grass. He worked a path through; each footstep sweeping sideways as well as forward, bending the sharp blades of nature's knives to the side. He stopped every five steps to listen. It was the only way to know if anything was in front of them. He could see only a few feet through the grass.

He stopped to listen: movement ahead, less than twenty feet away, coming towards them. The marine squad opened fire as they dropped into the slicing grass. The enemy, caught off guard by the sudden onslaught, returned fire, precious seconds late. The enemy's tracer bullets streaked through the darkness. Their red trails broke for a split second as they pierced the giant leaves, creating a strobe light of death. He couldn't tell the size of the enemy force. But the enemy's firepower was strong. There was no solid cover. The marines fired into the wall of grass from

The Marine moving into jungle grass; leaves like nature's knives; hard to penetrate in daylight or darkness.

prone positions, lying on the stalks that broke as the marines dropped for cover. The stalks pierced them like pungi sticks.

He thumbed his M-16 on full automatic for maximum fire power. The rapid bursts of fire held the enemy from advancing. The adrenaline rush pushed him into another dimension; everything slow motion; he could have touched the enemy tracers as they passed by his head.

"Blast where the tracers come from," he shouted, not knowing if he was heard above the deafening sound of the firefight. The enemy's return fire waned, and then stopped: three minutes of living hell was over. The enemy's moans drifted to them.

"Cover the flank," the enemy cried out; in English. Hell wasn't over.

"Cease fire!" the marine squad leader shouted. "Identify yourself!"

"Geronimo," resonated back through the darkness.

The squad leader radioed command base; call sign verified; another marine squad; a different platoon. The other marine squad had got twisted up, and crossed into the point man's sector.

"God: No! God: No!" the point man cried out. "Jesus: No! Please." He ran to the other squad. Marines lay twisted in the elephant grass. Some still held their weapons, some could not; no KIAs. One of the wounded called his name, one of his best friends through training; both came to country, assigned to different regiments.

"My God, My God, I almost killed my friend," he whispered.

"Are you hit?" the point man asked, feeling warm stickiness in his hands when they clasped in a hand shake.

"No; Just this damn jungle grass sliced me up pretty good," his friend said.

"We screwed up big time man. We got lost," his friend said. "We thought we heard something, and then we didn't. Then you guys opened fire. I was afraid we were going to die." He wouldn't let go of the point man's arm.

"We're all scared. It keeps us alive," the point man said. He wiped the blood from his friend's face and arms. "Nobody's dying. You'll be okay."

They heard the blades of thunder; choppers coming.

"God, take care of my friend over here," he said. They gripped each other's arm in farewell.

The point man ejected the half-empty clip from his rifle, and locked in a full one. He felt the mode button still on auto and flipped it back, wishing he could flip back time. He took deep breaths; blowing out slow through pursed lips as he moved to the front of the squad. The enemy now knew where they were. They still had to cross the valley.

He blocked his emotions. There was more to do.

CHAPTER 8

Where Are the Birds?

The marine squad moved across the small glade in their sweep up the valley. The point man had the right flank, the tree line next to him. Fresh footprints crossed the edge of the field. They spread out to push the enemy up the valley ahead of them. A lot like hunting with his family. They would see the hoof prints of the deer and spread out through the woods to drive it toward his brother or father who were waiting at the upper end of the valley.

Another marine unit acted as a blocking force at the end of this valley. He watched the tree line. No birds, no animals flushed ahead of them. Three months in-country, he never saw a bird or anything that looked like a squirrel or rabbit; unless he counted the rats; like the one that scampered cross his throat when he was sleeping. It was sad that that this beautiful land would not have abundant nature. It was the war; the constant bombardment, the firefights, the cloud of orange death. How long would it take to have them back after the fighting stopped?

He saw a flicker of movement in the tall grass ahead. He motioned the squad, his palm down moving it toward the ground as he dropped down and lay on the valley floor. The squad melted into the grass. The field stubble scraped his bare chest, his flak jacket unsnapped in the front because of the day's heat. The scent of the dry meadow so close, the feel of it against his body, brought a memory of home; of hard work that brought smiles as they hayed the field; a split second; then gone. He wanted to smile again. It had been so long.

The valley grass blocked the point man's view. He started crawling toward the place he had seen the flicker. The grass now became his advantage; he could move silently. He looked back at the squad. They followed in his path. The grass already bent over; their movement caused no break in the valley profile. They were undetectable if enemy eyes looked across the valley floor. He stopped to listen. He heard movement ahead then it stopped. He waited. The mosquitoes feasted on his face and bare arms. He didn't dare get up or brush them off. He pressed his head against his hands, squashing the horde between them; the respite short lived as more descended.

He moved forward, parting the grass with his hands before sliding ahead. The rustling in the grass came closer. He thumbed his rifle mode button to full auto. Sounds of rapid breathing: something was there. He strained to see around him. The grass exploded behind him. He spun his body, pointing his rifle to face the enemy. His radioman was in a battle; a yellow demon latched onto his hand. The enemy was a scraggly yellow dog.

The Edge of Enough

Shards of grass clung to the towel draped around the squad leader's neck. The organic tang now mixed with the metallic smell of blood and sweat. His body stung; slashed from forcing through razor-sharp elephant grass. Their patrol had started at dawn; the sun close to setting when they'd entered the compound tonight. He wiped his rifle and lay on his cot, the rifle next to him. Eight o'clock by his watch. He should wash the towel; should grab a shower, should eat something. He closed his eyes. Just a few minutes rest, that's what he wanted. Then he'd do all that other stuff.

Something brushed his cot. He opened his eyes; the hooch now cloaked in darkness. He had fallen asleep. His muscles tensed but he didn't move. When he was five or six years old, he'd slept in a room with four brothers, sharing a bed with his twin. When noises woke him in the night; he would keep his eyes closed and not move, afraid of the dark. It wasn't fear that kept him motionless now. It was the jungle in him, sorting out what and where the enemy was before he struck. A muffled noise under him: something crawled. Had VC infiltrated the compound? Or a beast? Please God, not another snake. His mind raced for options; his instinct took command. He slid his hand down the familiar shape of his rifle, his finger curled around the trigger. The movement under his cot stopped. He waited.

A swooshing sound outside; a flare launched into the night sky; the instant he needed. He leaped from the cot to the floor, his rifle pointed toward the movement under the cot. The flare popped. Light flooded the hooch. His trigger squeeze taut, he saw the dog lying under his cot, head on its paws, his own bush hat in the dog's mouth.

The dog had come to them when they were on an op in that valley six weeks ago: a puppy then, bone thin and starving. So desperate it had grabbed the radioman's hand to snatch a piece of beef jerky. Near death, still full of fight. The closest vill deserted, the puppy abandoned or lost.

He couldn't let him die. He'd tucked him into his shirt. He was point man for the squad then. The squad took turns carrying him on the op; against regulations: their secret. Back at the command base, they let the dog free. He hung around the squad. They took turns watching out for him. The pup came into the hooch a lot; a corner of the screen in the door made loose for him.

A lot changes in six weeks in this land of war. He was now squad leader and the starving puppy, a strong dog. Low growls sounded from between bared teeth, but the wagging tail gave away the dog's playful mood. The squad leader bent over and grabbed the hat. The dog hung on, sliding out with it. He picked him up. The dog dropped the hat, but lay still in his arm. "We're both gungy and hungry: time for a snack." The flare's light had depleted. He lit a candle, reached under his cot and pulled out his cardboard treasure box. He opened the flaps; the doors that led to the only touchable links to his home half a world away.

He grabbed the letters from her and tucked them next to the side of the box. He moved aside the camera, and the shiny watch band that reflected sunlight in the day and shimmered in the night. He had said he was looking for a darker band in a letter he wrote to his parents. His dad had sent him one: black; non reflective: Dad knew. The jeweler refused to take his dad's money knowing his son was at war. Pieces of folded wax paper lay near the end of the box. He should throw them away but couldn't. They had held homemade cookies and fudge she had made for him.

He spied what he wanted: Keebler cheese crackers: only one cracker left in the wrapper. He unfolded the cellophane and held the cracker in his hand. He broke it in half and gave one piece to the dog. He bit into the other half, the crisp crunch of the cracker softened from its time in the box, but the taste of the cheese delicious. His mouth watered in hunger and he started to push the rest into his mouth. His eyes locked onto the dog's face, now watching his: not begging, just watching. He broke a piece off, gave it to him and put the last of it in his flak jacket pocket to give him later.

He hadn't planned on getting so attached to the dog; he couldn't: none of the marines could. They would be going home. The dog was home. ARVNs in the base fed him sometimes and he'd hang out there when the squad was on missions. The dog would be okay. But he couldn't help feeling good when the dog picked his cot to rest under.

He had three more days before his turn to care for the dog ended, and then he would pass him to the radioman. It was going to be hard. He scratched the dog behind the ears. The dog took his hand in his mouth and just held it, gazing at him. "Ya, I like you too," the squad leader said.

He set the dog back on the floor and headed out of the hooch, curious about the flare that had been sent up. There was no response of rifle fire so he knew all was clear. He got to the perimeter wall. Three marines, the machine-gun team assigned to the squad, had come to see what had tripped the flare. They leaned on top of the sandbags looking into the concertina wire. Their helmets were set on the wall. They shared a smoke, squatting down below the wall to get a drag then handing it on. No one smoked above the wall, the glow a giveaway to their positions.

"What was the commotion?" he asked.

"Trip flare in the wire got set off. They sent up illumination to check it out: nothing there. Guess the flare just decided it had had enough and blew up. We all live on the edge of that feeling," the gunner said, and looked to the ground, unable to hold eye contact with the squad leader. He sat on his heels and took a drag from the dwindling cigarette. "You got any smokes?"

"The four that came from my c-rat meal; on the crate next to my cot." the squad leader said. He didn't smoke. He either traded with someone for the c-rat's chocolate paddy or gave them away.

The gun team headed for the hooch, toward his smokes. The squad leader moved further along the perimeter, his four-legged friend next to him. He came to the next watch position. He cleared his throat to let the marine know he was coming up on him. The marine sat on a stack of sandbags piled high enough so he could sit and see over the wall but not be a silhouette. A crumpled up ball of paper lay next to him.

"Making giant spitballs?" the squad leader asked.

"I wish," the marine said and started to pull and pinch the skin on his arm.

A friend of his in high school had done that. He had asked him why. "Final exam week, so much to deal with I don't know what to do." He had taken his friend to the Polka Dot, a local diner, and talked over coffee.

The squad leader had the same sense that the marine wanted to talk. "I could use some coffee. You got any?"

"There's some in my canteen."

The squad leader took a drink, passing the canteen back. He waited. They set in silence, watching the wire and taking turns at the coffee.

"Life's not fair you know," the watch marine blurted out. "Bad shit happens when you least expect it and can't be there to stop it." He pointed to the crumpled letter. "She doesn't want to wait for me. Says it's too long a time. I've got eight months to go. She's already gone out a couple of times. She's all I have. There's nothing to stick around for."

"I figured the spitball was bad news." The squad leader picked up the crushed ball of paper and smoothed it out. He turned it over. No writing on the back side. He handed it to the watch marine, blank side up. "Sometimes you can turn life around and start with a clean slate. She's as lonely as you. Use this and write her back tonight. Tell her why she should wait for you. See which side of the slate she picks."

The dog still lay by the squad leader's feet. The machine gunner had said that the flare had taken all it could and just blew. How much more could the watch marine take? He reached into his flak jacket pocket and pulled out the piece of cracker. The dog got to its feet, watching him. He picked him up and scratched him behind his ears. The dog leaned into his touch.

"Life isn't always fair, but sometimes it can be fixed with a little help," he whispered to the dog. He gave him the last piece of cracker and buried his face into the dog's fur, holding him close for a moment. Then he handed the dog to the watch marine. "Here. Now you've got something to stick around for. He likes cheese crackers: and likes his ears scratched. The dog is yours to care for until you get your answer."

He walked toward his hooch, not trusting himself to look back.

The Ten Percent Rule

The midmorning heat took its toll on the marine's squad as they crossed the valley floor. The sun beat down. Humidity: sauna thick. Chest-high elephant grass and scruff weeds: that's all that grew in this valley of Orange Death; no trees, no shade, just VC.

The twelve-man squad was the point for the platoon, with 2nd and 3rd Squads formed behind, at the flanks; a flying geese formation. The other two platoons, thirty-plus men each, were in their own grid, the mountain foothills on each side.

The Leader watched his men. One had stopped three times to drink water from another marine's canteen. The leader dropped back.

"Use your own water," he ordered.

"I'm out. I'll just take a little from the others," the man said, not able to meet the leader's eye. He had demonstrated irresponsibility before with the leader's squad, once bringing only one clip of ammo, and another time sleeping on the perimeter guard line at the Pass.

He checked the marine's canteens. Everybody was told to bring at least four. He had only two. Both empty.

"There's no way in hell that you should be out of water," he said. "How come they're empty?"

"They must have leaked out."

"Leaked out, my ass! You didn't fill 'em."

"With everything else, they'd be heavy."

"When, or if, you maggots become leaders, remember the 'Ten Percent Rule.' Ten Percent of your men will try to screw up the Marine Corps. Some of them will make it through basic and will be in your battlefield. Sort 'em out and get rid of them before they get somebody killed," said his boot camp drill instructor at Parris Island.

This man could not or would not, face the seriousness of combat. He had been assigned to base supply support before this op because of it. The lieutenant had wanted to give him another chance so here he was.

"You better pray resupply reaches us before you take much more from the others. We have a long way to go." They swept up the valley, the afternoon heat relentless. The marines moved slowly; the leader cautious. The valley was known for booby traps and land mines. Sporadic small-arms fire sounded to the north. The leader checked his map.

They had gone four miles: halfway to their mission target. "Take five," he said as he raised his arm, the signal to stop. They sat down, paired off, back to back to watch both directions, leaned against each other for support. No one paired with the marine who didn't bring water. He motioned him up and they sat back to back. He offered him some water.

"Just a little, and wash it around your mouth. It has to last," he said. The marine took a couple swallows, washed it around his mouth, then raised the canteen again and started glugging. The leader yanked the canteen from his hand.

"You don't give a damn about anybody but yourself. Change that or you've got a hard road ahead." He stood up so fast the other man fell backwards.

"Saddle up. We're moving out," he ordered the squad. They went another mile.

"Man down," his tail-end Charlie, the last man in the column, shouted.

The man who didn't bring water had collapsed. The leader radioed 2nd Squad for the corpsman. The man was conscious but pale; mild heat exhaustion. They elevated his feet, putting them on his helmet. The leader took out his canteen and sprinkled water on the man's face then wet his towel and put it under the back of the man's neck.

The corpsman got there with a three-man rifle team from the other squad.

"Dump your water on him, soak him down. I'm calling in a medevac," the corpsman told the squad. They took out their canteens and started to wet the man down. The man looked only at the corpsman, not the squad, as he turned to his side to avoid their glances.

"Put your canteens away." the leader ordered.

"He needs water to cool down," the corpsman said.

"He needs to learn to bring his own water."

"He may die before they get him back," the corpsman said.

"He knew the consequences: his choice."

They heard the medevac chopper coming. The other squads were getting close.

"He's yours, corpsman," the leader said. "1st Squad, move out."

The leader looked west, up the valley. He saw the F-4 Phantom jets streaking down from high in the sky; saw their payload blast into the mountain that rose up at the end of the valley. The screams of their engines reached him fifteen to twenty seconds later; after they had soared back into the sky, lining up for another pass. The air strike target was his platoon's destination.

"Do a good job guys. We're on our way." he said, crossing himself. He moved the squad toward the foothills at the end of the valley. The danger he had left behind, no less than that ahead.

CHAPTER 9

The Child Within

The dog-tag and crucifix swung from leather ties around the squad leader's neck. He adjusted his jungle boot, pulling the laces snug; his other dog-tag tucked between the lace and the boots tongue.

"You keep one dog-tag around your neck so the corpsman knows what type of blood is spilling from your gut and the other on your boot so they know which piece goes with whom and they can piece you back together. You WILL finish the firefight:" words barked at them by his drill instructor back at Parris Island; then followed by the instructor's diabolical laugh. He thought then it was a crude joke. He knew now it wasn't. He gave one last pull to tighten the lace and knotted it.

He sat on the sandbag wall next to the squad's hooch at command base. His bare chest pressed his writing pad against his knee. It was the first chance he'd had to get off a letter in over a week. He took the writing paper and started his letter; to her. "Hi my love, all is well. I miss you…. I miss your smile. I miss you making me laugh; like that time at the bottom of the Gorge when we had sat and planned our future together, then drove on the logging trail back to the main road; the cars lights off, not wanting to break the aura of the night. 'Please keep your lights off as you exit the theater'; your words. I miss the way you scolded me for stealing a kiss in broad daylight at the A & W drive-in diner, even though I know you could have stopped me. I miss the way you bring out the child in me…."

The mid-morning sun already hot, his sweat smudged the words. There was no way to escape the heat. He kept writing. He had to stop a few times, his thoughts going back to their last mission. He shook his head to clear his mind; only good news home; then started writing again. "We had a great birthday party for the newbie in the squad; just turned eighteen. We scrounged up party favors and two twelve-inch candles and cookies from a two-week-old care package, some with furry blue-green spots on the edges. The candles bent over in the heat. I took a few flicks of the party. They'll be in the roll of film I'm sending you. We did games. Knife and hatchet throwing, wrestling and pillow fights with half-filled sand bags. Not everyday party games. But we're not everyday kids. Ha-ha."

He stopped writing; the last few words refusing to leave his mind. The truth in them screamed at him. They were all battle hardened. Some were rough spoken, and some quoted Shakespeare. A couple were over six foot six with shoulders as wide as a barn door, one of them about five foot two and his frame so thin he couldn't cast a shadow on a sunny day. All grown men: on the outside. But he knew them on day patrols when they prayed to make it back; he knew their voices grew softer as they spoke about loved ones back home; and their laughter boomed as they sang "Itsy-Bitsy-Spider" as the monsoon rains poured down on them.

He knew them at night on ambushes; when he heard their whispered prayers to please take care of their mom and dad. Grown men on the outside, jungle hard, ready to do battle with the enemy; but children on the inside; wanting to have birthday parties and play games. To skinny-dip in the slow-moving streams on a hot summer day; to be at a beach party with friends, toasting marshmallows over a fire and holding hands with their young love as the silver moon rose over the lake.

He went back to writing the letter again. He wrote another page then signed off, folding the letter and sticking it into an envelope. He jumped down from the wall, went to his hooch and took out the roll of film from his camera and put it in with the letter. He licked the flap carefully. This was his last envelope. They were headed for the mountain tomorrow. A search-and-destroy mission. They had fought on that mountain before. A chill went through his body. He needed to get the letter in the mail bag tonight; the child within would be gone tomorrow.

The Kodak Pictures

Wild men held at bay by soft women on stage. Familiar songs sung in foreign voices. Short skirts; gyrating bodies: wolf whistles and hoots. The squad leader sat on the ground with the marine platoon at their forward command base, his rifle across his lap. They watched the USO show. He looked around him. The mountain pass loomed behind them, a formidable backdrop. Uneasiness swept through him. In and beyond the mountains, the enemies purge the villages and we're watching people dance and sing. It didn't feel right.

"You need a break," the captain had told them. Maybe it was true. The squad leader took out his Kodak pocket camera. His Love had sent him film.

"Send me pictures of you," she had requested.

He had sent her other flicks. Of happy things, of their day patrols that showed huts on the edges of the paddies and soulful pagodas that stood alone in a squared patch of red earth, and banana trees, their green fruit growing upside down, and pictures taken on a mountain ledge over the spacious valley below, calm and serene. He had sent her flicks of Vietnamese farmers working in the paddies, pant legs rolled up above their knees, water buffalo standing nearby.

The Marines' hooch at forward fire base.

But never of the blood: or the bodies: or the terror in the eyes of children that searched for their mama-son after a VC attack: and not the agony on a marine's face as he held a fallen warrior. She would see that on the Six O'clock News, over and over.

Twenty-four flicks to a film. No do overs. He started clicking the marines around him, the singers on stage, and the afternoon sun illuminating the dark green of the mountains. He clicked and wound the lever forward twenty times and then held the camera facing him. He thought of her, smiled and took a flick of himself; then wound it to twenty-one.

He'll take the rest later and mail it out with a letter tomorrow. He put the camera back in his pocket.

The loud urgent wail of the siren blasted over the compound, drowning out the sounds of music. The marines jumped to their feet; firefight somewhere; whose unit would be choppered out? The captain's messenger ran to the microphone.

"Third Platoon, fall out, Choppers coming, LZ in five minutes," he yelled. The squad leader slung his rifle over his shoulder and ran to his hooch. He grabbed his gear and turned to leave for the LZ then remembered the camera. There would be no good flicks where they were going. He took it from his pocket and placed it in the cardboard

The marine's unit preparing to lift off on rapid response assault mission.

box next to his homemade fudge, from her. He ran toward the choppers knowing that whatever happened, the last flick on the Kodak was of him, smiling.

CHAPTER 10

The Swimming Hole

The twelve marines sweltered under the midday heat; the temperature felt over a "buck"; air thick and heavy; their bodies drenched with sweat. They had been doing night acts followed by day patrols for two weeks straight; no relief: The platoon short of men. No questions: no whining: just doing the work. They had not made contact with, nor even seen the enemy in those two weeks. They were getting tired, complacent,

and edgy. The marine squad moved across the open terrain. The point man raised his hand with a clenched fist, and dropped to one knee; the signal of eminent danger.

The squad leader scanned their surroundings. Years ago it might have been a village. No hooches left here now, just partially destroyed pagodas, a few rangy scrub trees and dying banana trees. He moved up to the front of the squad. A bomb crater, fifteen to twenty feet wide, lay ahead; in the middle of piles of rubble: a setup for a VC ambush. Clumps of earth the size of basketballs scattered across the ground, the only cover for the marines. He signaled the machine-gun team up. He pumped his arm up and down with closed fist; the signal to hurry. He would move with them, straight toward the crater with the second fire team. He signaled the first fire team to the right flank, the third fire team to the left flank. He moved them up in leap-frog movements, one team at a time. Move up a few yards; drop to the ground; next team move up: they closed in on the edge of the rubble. No enemy fire. The squad leader's team climbed over the rubble. He signaled the other teams to wait and cover them. They needed to check for booby traps.

The team checked around the rubble and the crater. No enemy: no traps: just a bomb crater filled with water. The squad leader signaled the others up. The rubble gave them more protection than the open terrain. He positioned the men around the crater. No enemy could surprise them. He motioned over the radioman and called in their coordinates to command base. They would take rest here for a while.

He walked up to the edge. He couldn't see into the murky water. He had swum in water like this on hot summer days; none the worse for it. He came from a dying mill town. No town pool. He and his brothers and sister swam in the river and the brooks that flowed down the valley; the river muddy after a rain, the brooks always goose-bump cold. He took a drink from his canteen; remembering the fun of the swimming and floating in old tire inner-tubes in the river. The idea of a swimming party flashed into his mind: time off from war.

"Anyone up for a swim party?" he asked.

"Man, that's full of leeches," the radioman said.

"Hell I'm game if you are," the point man said to the squad leader.

The squad laughed, not thinking the leader would do it.

"Every second man from him, stand watch," the squad leader said. He pointed to the radioman. "The rest, that want to, can start the party; fifteen minutes, then you switch with the watch teams," he said. "Watch teams, stay sharp," he ordered.

He pulled off his helmet, flak jacket and ammo; took his lighter and compass from his trouser pocket, and laid them next to his rifle. He left his trousers and boots on. He stuck his bush hat on his head. "The man that comes out with the most leeches wins," he said and walked into the crater. He slipped on the muck and went under. He swam back to the surface and heard their laughter. He spit out the mouthful of brown water and swam to other side: only one leech: sucked onto his stomach: and one on his left bicep. The rest of the designated men stripped down and jumped in: some stripped naked.

These man–boys shed the weeks of mental stress, and physical drain; replacing it with cheerfulness and exuberance: an escape from the reality of war: if only for a moment. They all got their chance to swim. The radioman pulled out a bar of Ivory soap from his flak jacket pocket. They cut it up, washed up; clothes included.

"Move out in fifteen minutes," the squad leader ordered. "You win with eight leeches," he said and pointed to the machine gunner. He tossed him a mini cigarette pack that he took from his c-rats. The point man came out of the water; soap lather concentrated on an area that was physically excited.

"Hey; the soap is ninety-nine percent pure: looks like the one percent found something tiny that wasn't pure," the squad leader said. The squad hooted their agreement. He checked his map. They had been here for an hour. Their patrol was more than half completed before they had stopped. He knew it was time well spent. The men were refreshed; in body; and mind.

"The lieutenant for you, "the radioman said. He handed him the handset. The men knew he was getting chewed out for being stopped for so long.

"We've made good progress, Sir. We stopped and cleared out possible booby traps in an open area; underneath the surface: Made of a pointed, worm-like substance that would stick to the men. No sir. We destroyed them. Thank you. I'll pass that along to them," he said. "Yes sir: in a crater; leeches. ETA: three hours. Yes sir; in time for dinner. The squad leader smiled. The lieutenant approved of the decision to stop and swim. And he had a sense of humor. He handed the handset back to the radioman.

"The lieutenant said you've earned the swim; and to make sure the leech marks are clean."

"Squad, saddle up. Keep boxcar width between you. Three hours to dinner," he said. He looked at the crater full of water; the terrain all around: dry. Swimming there had renewed the men's spirit.

"More than a crater of water," he whispered.

He signaled to the point man.

"Move out," he ordered.

The squad crossed over the rubble: into the war.

You Don't Have To Like It

The squad leader squatted down to look under the building. This was not his favorite part of coming out of the bush for a few days' rest; burning out the latrine barrels. "If it's something that has to be done, just do it. You don't have to like it": words from his father that echoed in his mind. He reached in with the iron hook and snared the fifty-five-gallon metal drum that had been cut in half; and dragged it out from under the latrine. Half full or half empty, there was no positive way to describe the odor. It was crap. He pushed an empty drum back in its place. Hand holds were cut out of each side. The marine helping him was nowhere in sight. "It's a long road that doesn't have a turn in it," his dad would say. He made a mental note: pay-back would come later.

He pulled his leather gloves tight and gripped the side holes, picking up the drum of feces and carried it to the burn area, three car lengths away. He poured a couple gallons of diesel fuel in then took a piece of burlap bag, lit it with his lighter and dropped it in the drum. Black putrid smoke curled up into the air. He stopped and took a drink from his canteen, looking across the compound for his helper. Three drums done: seven more to go before chow time.

No c-rations for the next few days. Here they had mess hall food. He had gone to breakfast. Real eggs; anyway you wanted them as long as that was scrambled. Thick rind bacon; the grease running on the paper plate, waiting to be wiped clean with buttered toast; and mashed potato, left over from last evening's meal, formed into patties and browned on the grill. Breakfast almost like at hunting camp back home.

He had a breakfast like this the morning he shot his first buck. He had climbed the mountain pass that morning; a hard climb. The morning fog became thick. He'd found the spot he wanted; a deer path around the base of a ledge. He set in to wait. He was there to put food on the table for a family of eight. "God, just bring the one you want me to harvest," he prayed. He saw something through the fog; then didn't. Then it was there: running toward him; fast; close. The buck held his head high, showing a chandelier of antlers. He raised his rifle; and fired. The deer ran past him then dropped to the ground. He went to it. The buck was passed his prime; his muzzle gray, a film over his eyes hinting at blindness coming. That might have been why the deer had not seen him. A magnificent animal lay at his feet, its life taken by him. He had felt nauseous.

The roar of an F-4 Phantom jet streaking above the compound brought his thoughts back. He raised the canteen over his head and poured water on himself as if trying to wash away the memory. Sometimes in his sleep or quiet moments during the day, he saw the deer; the sadness still deep within him. He had been in firefights; enemy had died. He had walked up to them as they lay on the ground, their life taken. He felt no regrets; except for that time on the mountain ledge. Yet he still carried remorse for the deer. He had tried to figure it out. The closest explanation of the difference why for him; the firefights were war, kill or be killed; the enemy skilled, armed with weapons of war and an agenda of destruction. But the enemy could make choices. They chose to be destroyers. The deer was innocent; its only agenda, life: no choices.

He put the cap back on the canteen as he looked across the compound; help still nowhere to be seen. He reached down, picked up the hook and headed to the next drum. He had learned not everyone could do what had to be done.

CHAPTER II

Hidden Death

The squad leader climbed into the back of the supply convoy truck headed to a base south of Da Nang. He looked at his watch; 0800. He got back from a night action two hours ago. He dropped his travel pack onto the floor next to his feet. He wasn't sure what was ahead of him. The lieutenant called it an information-sharing think-tank; he called it

a show-and-tell class on booby traps. He might be the only bush marine there; maybe the only NCO, the rest officers. The mission was still the same; destroy or disrupt the enemy. But in a different way than he was used to: this time by talk.

The convoy drove two hours; no stops; no slowdowns. He saw vills in the distance. Kids waited at the road's edge and waved to the convoy as it passed. They knew it wouldn't stop. The marines riding shotgun threw them packages of gum and candy bars. The kids swarmed to get them after the convoy passed; a prize for them in this war-torn land. Most so young they had no idea what peace and plenty was. They were born in war; lived in war; knew nothing else. The squad leader's heart felt heavy. He wanted peace for them: and he wanted this day over so he could go back to the bush and do his specialty. There he could see and feel the difference they made. His hands gripped his rifle; his knuckles white. He wanted to be in action; not talking.

He got to the base, assigned to a barracks; meetings start in one hour. He had no notes.

"What they want is real-time experience to share with others that are just headed into the bush," the lieutenant had said. You don't get experience talking about it, the squad leader thought.

He tossed his pack in a locker and kept his rifle, helmet and flak jacket. He removed the ammo clip from his rifle and put it in his flak jacket. The base was huge; the size of a small town. He passed a cafeteria, and a building marked "Mail," even a PX. The clothing building was bigger than the Rockdale Discount Store in the city next to his hometown. Jeeps and half-tracks and convoy trucks charged up and down the street; part dirt, part hard pack or tar; he wasn't sure which: different than his forward base with sandbagged bunkers and perimeter walls. He headed to the meeting.

The squad leader entered the meeting room and stopped just beyond the doorway. Most there were marines; some ARVNs. Eyes turned toward him, the buzzing hum of talk quieted. He noticed most were dressed in pressed fatigues, shined jungle boots: no helmet: no flak jacket: no rifle. He stepped sideways and positioned himself with his back to the wall, mentally noting the exit door; not out of fear, but instinct. He slung his rifle, with its rope sling, on his right shoulder; barrel down. The clack it made when it brushed the ammo clip in his flak jacket carried across the room.

A tall man with grayish hair strode from the podium in front toward him. The others made way for him. He moved with the confidence of a man befitting the oak leaf cluster he wore on the lapel of his shirt; a major. The squad leader started to salute him.

"You can pass on the salute today, corporal. We are here to salute what you men do in the bush," the major said. He extended his hand. "You can leave your rifle with my aide. Grab a coffee and come with me to the side room. We'll talk a little before we get started."

The squad leader walked to the table with the coffee. Plain china cups: with saucers. Baskets with donuts and Danishes and fruits filled the table next to the coffee. He poured his coffee; kept it black; grabbed two sugar donuts and walked into the side room. His rifle he kept slung. The major waited to close the door. He noticed the squad leader still carried the rifle. He smiled as he closed the door.

The major explained the reason for the meeting. The incidence numbers for booby trap casualties were high: due to inexperience, down-played danger; and haste. The squad leader had seen some of this first hand.

"Your work today is to relay how to detect and avoid the traps. It will be mostly Q & A. Say what you need to; tell us what we need to know," the major said. He stood and gripped the corporal's shoulder. "You will save lives today," he said.

The squad leader didn't respond. He thought back to his feelings about getting experience by doing, not talking. He realized he had been wrong. When he first came to country, his squad leader had taught him by telling. They were right. It was better to learn by other people's mistakes; to avoid making your own. The major led him to the podium.

He stood in the silence for a moment to gather his thoughts. He told them about the mission when the scout and his dog led the platoon. They walked off the trail to go around a fallen tree. The dog stopped. He wouldn't move; just looked back at the scout. The scout noticed dying leaves on grass and ferns. He called his dog back and probed the ground with a stick. The stick went through the false top: Pungi pit; stakes with sharpened end pointed upwards; covered with feces. They would have pierced his jungle boots and legs. The scout was on his second tour; knew his work well, yet, if not for the dog, would not have seen it: the enemy was skilled in this type of warfare.

The squad leader told them to look for un-natural things: fresh dirt on old ground: dying, yellow leaves next to those green and growing: and to look for the too natural: no marks for a short distance on a used trail: and not to move objects; cooking pots; straw thatched doors lying on the ground; disposed U.S. armament leaning against the trail. The squad leader realized they could talk for hours and still miss things.

The meeting went for four hours; no break the interest so high. The major suggested they wrap it up. The squad leader had sat down in the crowd after his Q & A session and listened to others. He needed to add something. He raised his hand.

"A three-year-old baby-son played next to a path on a paddy dike. The trip wire he moved set off a VC booby trap that took his right leg. We never heard if he lived or died. An elderly mama-son walked into the paddy to work the seedling rice, not seeing the VC trip wire under the surface of the paddy water. She had raised her family there, worked the fields and paddies all her life. We ran a patrol through their vill a week after it happened. The vill mourned for her. The enemy doesn't care about the civilians who detonate their traps nor do they care if the traps are placed in or around a vill. The civilians will be left to care for themselves after this war. What are we doing to help them, besides praying for them?" he asked. The major took the question himself.

"We need to do more but we are aware of it. We work with the Civil Action Program, working with ARVN counterparts," he said. "We can address this further at the next meeting."

The major took a few questions then adjourned the meeting. The squad leader walked to the door he had come in. The major stopped him.

"Find a bunk in your barracks area. I've cleared you to stay two more days. We have people who want to hear more," he said.

The Rock of Salvation

The shells made a rushing sound coming in, exploding on impact, changing the very outline of the earth. The twelve-man squad dove under a house-sized rock when the first one came. Two more followed right behind, their blasts driving the marines further back under the rock.

"We're taking incoming, heavy stuff, sir; coming from the east," the squad leader shouted to his lieutenant over the radio. Two more rounds hit beyond the rock, the force of the blast showered them in dirt and stones. He didn't know the enemy had shells this damaging. Three more rounds hit into the ground, their blasts circled the rock. He recognized the pattern; they had been zeroed in. Next would be fire-for-effect.

Somehow, the enemy knew where they were. He ordered the men to move as far back as they could. The next shell shattered off part of the rock. He didn't know how many more direct hits it could sustain. "We can't take much more, lieutenant," he yelled in the handset.

"You're taking fire from a U.S. Navy Destroyer," the lieutenant said. "HQ's on it."

"Shut 'em down, Sir. Shut 'em down: they're ready to fire-for-effect, damn it!"

The naval ship had not been informed of the marines' position. The squad had set off movement-monitoring sensors that were embedded on the island. The destroyer was firing its big (five inch) guns on the marines. They were a forgotten squad.

Three more shells came in, two fell short of the rock; the third one's blast demolished part of the top.

"Don't move," the squad leader said. Their only hope was for the destroyer's gunners to think they had neutralized their target.

The shelling stopped. Silence: only the sound of the squad's breathing. A marine started to turn over. The leader held his arm up with a closed fist; don't move. Ten minutes passed, an eternity for them. The squad's radioman held out the handset to the leader. "You're clear, the ship knows it's you," the lieutenant said.

The marines were part of a search-and-destroy operation to locate and push part of a VC regiment to the other side of the island into a blocking force of ROK marines.

The squad moved out from under the rock, shaking off dirt and stone from their bodies; trauma from their mind. They moved out, focused on their mission. The squad leader stopped to look back at their salvation. It stood tall, re-shaped by war, but steadfast; its character unchanged. He looked north, toward the eminent battle.

"Lord, I pray we're as strong as your rock."

CHAPTER 12

A Ton of Trouble

The marine's squad started across the rice paddies, walking on the earthen dike that sliced between them. The dike was five feet wide, a hundred yards long with murky paddy water on each side. It led into a thick tree line that separated the paddies from a vill. No way around: no cover: twelve men in the open: a nightmare comes true.

"Point man, third rifleman; make 'em full auto," the squad leader ordered. The two men switched their rifles to full automatic; immediate

fire power if needed. "Big guns; at the ready," he commanded the M-60 machine-gun team. "Spread out; box car room."

They moved a third of the way across. The point man dropped to one knee, hand held up with closed fist; the signal of imminent danger. The squad went to kneeling firing position. Each rifleman covered alternate fields of fire to the one in front of him. The last man covered the rear. The squad leader moved up to his point man.

"Gook squatting in the paddy, next to the dike," the point man said. The squad leader saw him. No weapon: but you can't see booby traps.

"Spot me fifty feet then bring on the squad. Watch the tree line," he told the point man. He moved forward, intent on the figure in the paddy and the terrain. He looked for fresh turned dirt; a glimmer of wire; anything not normal: or too normal.

He had gone the fifty and sensed the squad's movement behind him. The figure in the paddy jumped onto the dike. The squad leader aimed his rifle at his chest, finger curled around the trigger: Still no weapon. But

the figure was a boy, about six or seven. It was hard to tell ages here. He saw the boyish face, inquisitive not afraid; and the spindly legs of youth.

"La-di; la-di," he shouted to the boy: "come here; come here." The young boy turned and yelled toward the vill. The marines dropped into the paddy, tight against the dike, weapons at the ready. Crashing sounds came from the tree line. A bull water buffalo burst through the trees and into the paddy. His horns, tip to tip, wider than a person's outstretched arms; man-tall at the shoulders. His massive head held high; nostrils flared as he drew in the scent of the marines. The bull ranged back and forth in the paddy water; getting closer and more agitated.

The squad leader had seen water buffalo pulling tillers to turn the ground over before rice was planted. He had seen them saddled with baskets of wood. He knew they were the families' work horse, their tractor, their watch dog. He did not want to kill it.

"De-de; de-de mou," he yelled to the child, pointing to the bull: leave; leave now. The boy started to laugh. His prank had stopped the marines.

"Guns up," the squad leader commanded. The machine-gun team ran to the front, set up onto the edge of the dike. They waited for the fire order. The bull was fifty yards out, head lowered, mouth frothing; two thousand pounds of trouble.

The squad leader saw the boy's face change from fun to fear: his pet about to be killed. The boy tried to wave the bull off, and gave a piercing whistle. The bull, too intent to hear, charged the marines.

"Spray a burst next to him," the squad leader commanded the gunner.

"I can drop him," the gunner said, anxiety in his voice.

Don't touch him till I tell you to."

The gunner fired a ten-second burst. Finger-sized bullets, six hundred rounds per minute, pierced the paddy. The eruption of water and mud sprayed the bull's side. It turned away and stopped; chest heaving; confused. The boy whistled again. The bull turned and ran back to him and lowered its head. The boy reached up, grabbed one of its horns and led him off the paddy. He got to the end of the dike and motioned with his hand toward the vill. The bull ran back into the trees.

"Nice shooting." The squad leader slapped the gunner's helmet as he walked past. "Now let's get the hell out of this paddy." He moved the

squad to the tree line; the boy waited at the edge. The squad leader stopped in front of him. He saw the trauma in the boy's eyes. He took out a partial pack of Keebler cheese crackers, sent from his Love, and put four crackers in the boy's hand. He put the last two into the boy's other hand and motioned toward the trees where the bull had disappeared. The boy smiled, nodded and ran to give the treat to his pet.

"What the hell was that all about," the point man asked.

"I had a puppy when I was nine; Tracker. I couldn't save him from the car that hit him; but we could save this kid's pet." The squad leader raised his arm and motioned the squad forward.

CHAPTER 13

Phantoms on the Ridge

The candle light illuminated the marine sprawled on the cot, muddied jungle boots off his feet, trousers still on, shirtless under his open flak jacket. The door was quiet on its leather hinges as a messenger entered the hut. He reached to wake him, freezing as the man's hand darted from under the flak jacket, steel flashing from the knife he held in the candlelight. The man was on his feet facing the intruder, determining, friend or foe. Recognition came through his sleep-deprived eyes; the marine put his Ka-Bar back in its sheath and sat down on his cot.

"Tell them I'll be there in five." He glanced at his watch as he pulled on his boots. He heard the choppers coming in, their ride to where? Time check: 2200.

In-flight briefing; two F-4 Phantom jets crashed on the side of a mountain. The fate of two pilots and their systems operator was unknown. Mission directive; locate the airmen, bring them back. The choppers flew between the mountain ridges. The men could see the fire from the impact site. They stood with rifles locked and loaded as the chopper neared the ground, hovering low. At their leader's signal, they jumped into the carnage below, the chopper lifting away into the night. Time check: 2225.

Two squads formed perimeter outposts beyond the impact site. He and the 3rd Squad started to search for the airmen. A shudder ran through his body, seeing the aircraft pieces scattered down the smoldering mountainside.

The search team found remnants of a cockpit, still burning, the pilot's body strapped in his seat, the systems operator's seat behind the pilot, empty. He whispered a quiet prayer, his mind flashing back to the in-flight briefing. *"Locate the airmen or enough body parts to verify four separate bodies."* Time check: 2300 hrs.

Commands issued; remove the pilot, prepare him for extraction; keep searching for the other three. His mind pictured what the pilot would have been doing a few hours ago; writing a quick letter home, telling them that all is quiet and well, how much he loved and missed them and he would be home soon. The marine cursed. Which would get home first, his letter or his coffin?

Outposts report enemy movement along the top of the ridge; they were ordered to engage. The night wore on. Sporadic rifle fire coming from all the outposts verified the enemy's desire to access the site. The search squad had found the partial remains of two more airmen. One left to find. Time check: 0200.

They were almost through the crash site. He glimpsed a metallic flash in the brush. He shouted a warning to the men as he thumbed the button on his M–16 for full automatic. He felt the steel of the trigger, the weapon ready to unleash its deadliest strength. He held his fire, target still not verified. He moved forward. In the smoldering vegetation, cradled by the trees, he saw the burned, broken body of the fourth airman, his wedding ring glimmering in the firelight; its last request: we've given our all; take us home.

Daylight had come. Mission completed. No one left behind. The marine was back on his cot, still dressed, just his boots off. His eyes flickered under his closed eyelids, searching for peace. A letter just scribbled to his loved one lay next to him, saying "All is quiet and well: I miss you: I love you: I'll be home soon." Time check....

CHAPTER 14

Only Way Out

"Lock and load, we're going in." the squad leader commanded. The marines slammed their ammo clips into their rifles. The noise resonated inside the chopper, the tension high. The chopper dove down toward the jungle clearing. The rear door opened as it descended, side gunners ready to open fire with the fifty-caliber machine guns, praying they

would not be needed. Adrenalin surged through the squad leader's veins, the readiness for the fight at its peak inside him. The chopper flew into the clearing, five feet above the ground.

"Go! Go! Go," the squad leader yelled, and jumped. There was no time to land the chopper, not knowing if the enemy waited. The eleven-man squad followed him. He counted the men as they jumped to the ground beside him and then raised his arm in a circular motion, the signal for the pilot to lift up. The pilot crossed himself and then pointed back to him. The chopper's engines screamed to full power as it lifted up over the treetops: The marines' insertion complete; their life-line now disappearing over the jungle canopy.

"Move out," he ordered pointing north into the tree line; away from the clearing. He pumped his fist up and down: hurry. He took one last look toward the chopper, now just a dark speck in the sky. He felt the knot tighten in his stomach. It did every time: Being left....

They entered the jungle, into the enemy's domain. He focused on the mission, the knot in his stomach subsided. He took out his compass and made the azimuths for the extraction point coordinates, then set it. The choppers would pick them up at those coordinates in four days, their only way out. That's when the knot in his stomach would come back.

It wouldn't be there as they listened for the blades of thunder come up the valley for them after their mission was done. It wouldn't be there as he popped the smoke grenade to let the pilot know it was them. The knot would come as they ran to board the hovering chopper. That's when hidden enemy would strike; when the squad's backs were to the tree line, when they were the most vulnerable. The knot would be there as he watched the chopper's machine gunners as the squad ran toward them. Their eyes would tell him if the enemy was behind him. A heartbeat before they jumped in the chopper, he would know if they made it ... then the knot would go ... until the next mission.

The Death Letter

The marine's squad leader looked from the window openings of the chopper. He saw their Cobra gunship escorts on each side. They flew high over the island and seemed to pass it. The pilot gave him a nod, holding up two fingers.

"Two minutes; lock and load. We're going in," the marine said. He reached to his left-side shirt pocket and felt his wallet, wrapped in plastic. Nothing in it except two letters that he always carried: one; from her: the other; his death letter.

He wrote it the night their position was mortared. He took the packing paper from the box of her home-made fudge. He ripped part of it off; small so he could carry it in his wallet. The real truth being he would have written forever of his love for her. He wrote of his promise to her: I won't get hurt. I'll be back and we will spend the rest of our lives together. The letter said he was so sorry that he couldn't keep that promise. God had other plans for them. The letter told her that he loved her more than life itself. He filled the front and went to the back side of the paper. He wrote smaller because he had so much more to tell her.

It was hard to write. His tears blinded him. He got near the bottom; so much more to say. He wrote up the edges until all the paper was full. They always ended their letters to each other with: Love You Forever and a Day. He got to the last of the paper ending with: Love You Forever. The Day was gone.

The gunships abruptly changed direction and thundered toward the edge of the island near the river junction, the bright mid-morning sun at their back. They strafed the tree lines and tall grass with M-60 turret guns and 40mm grenade launchers. The chopper with the twelve-man marine squad on board angled back toward the island, and came in fast, swooping to the clearing; an iron eagle after prey. The marines jumped out the back. The side gunners blasted the tree line with their fifty-caliber guns to keep the enemy back. It lifted up and out as the marines gave cover fire from the ground.

"On me," the squad leader commanded and moved forward to engage the enemy.

He reached into his left-side shirt pocket and felt the wallet; the letters still safe.

CHAPTER 15

Mission on the Bridge

The squad leader on the bridge couldn't make out the object in the river; early morning fog over the water: Nature's camouflage. It floated along the shore, at times snagging onto fallen trees along the edge, holding for a while, then breaking loose; the slow-moving current freeing it to continue on toward the bridge. It looked like a log; yet different. He moved sideways, searching for a break in the misty haze. He pushed his rifle's safety button to off; his orders: shoot anything that floated toward the bridge; the possibility of hidden explosives high.

"Got something in the water," he yelled to the squad on watch with him. He kept his rifle sights trained on it as it drifted closer. "It's a body," he yelled.

He waited, the corpse still targeted, his finger on the trigger. The object had been hard to identify as a person; bloated beyond description; black pajamas on the torso stretched beyond the limit; now shredded. He couldn't shoot: not into a person already dead.

His mom and dad had taken him and his siblings to the cemetery at times, usually around Easter, to take care of the graves of family that had died. They planted fresh flowers or refreshed the ground around ones starting to bloom again. They would walk between the plots, careful not to step on someone's grave. His mom had said they needed to show respect for the dead. They had earned it.

If he allowed the body to reach the bridge the marines could be killed and the bridge destroyed. He scanned the river bank between the floater and the bridge; lots of dead branches from trees that had been cleared back for security purposes.

"Keep your eyes on the body. I'm going down to the water. Notify the lieutenant," he ordered the squad's radioman. He ran to the end of the bridge. Four Vietnamese locals were on the road and followed him. They got to the river's edge; the body still fifty to sixty yards upriver, the distance between telephone poles back home. He grabbed a dead tree branch that lay on the ground, motioning the others to bring more. He speared the branches into the murky river bottom, forming a make-shift fence where the body would drift. He didn't know if it would work, but there would still be time for the squad to shoot before it got too close. He went back up to the road, having the locals come with him. The body floated closer; the arms bumped against the shore. It made a slow spin as if it was trying to help guide itself into place and then it gently nudged up against the spear barrier. It stopped; now held by the wood obstacles: The marines and bridge safe; the corpse respected.

He went back on the bridge. The lieutenant and engineers were there, now headed toward him. His squad's watch ending; their relief now in place, he stayed to report to the lieutenant.

"Why didn't you shoot it?" the lieutenant demanded.

"I felt it was too close to the bridge and the men on it; I thought it would be safer to stop it in case," he said. He wasn't comfortable with the half-truth. "Lieutenant, I didn't want to shoot a man already dead unless I absolutely had to, sir," he said.

The lieutenant said nothing, just watched him for a moment. "Would you if you had to?" the lieutenant asked.

"If there were no alternative, I would sir," the squad leader said.

"Honest answer. Go get some rest," the lieutenant said.

"The body's clear; no booby traps," the engineer yelled up from the river.

The squad leader heard this and felt relief. He had made the right decision. "Thank you God," he whispered. He headed off the bridge.

He walked into his hooch, took off his gear, and then lay on the cot. He thought of his Love, praying he would dream of her lying next to him; her lips putting gentle kisses on his: But he knew the dream would be of the body. He wondered where it had drifted from and would the family ever be able to visit the grave; his last thoughts as he drifted to sleep.

The Marine at a friendly vill as the squad takes a rest break.

The squad leader bounded from the cot, now standing, rifle in hand. He had been asleep, coming off bridge watch two hours earlier. The commotion in camp woke him. It grew in intensity; people yelling; voices in Vietnamese; some in English. He stepped outside the hooch. The activity came from the other side of the bridge. He needed sleep but grabbed his flak jacket and helmet and went toward the ruckus. The marine's platoon had been assigned to relieve the bridge security two days ago. His unit had just come off a four-week search-and-destroy op in the mountains. This was going to be a week-long rest break. Guard duty at night; two hours on, two hours off; but only a three-hour guard duty during the day.

He crossed the bridge and stopped next to the relief squad's leader.

"What's going on?" he asked.

"Word is we are going back into the bush tomorrow, no rest break. Some of the guys are mad as hell. Guess they got used to cots and having someone do their laundry and it only took two days for some of them to get spoiled." he said.

The squad leader went back to his hooch. He wanted to write his Love. It would be a while before he got another chance, if the rumor was true. He reached into his pack for his writing paper and felt the letters he had there from her. One from weeks ago: he carried a letter from her; always. The other three had just reached him when he got to the bridge. He took them out and re-read them; slowly. Her voice resonated within him; he could smell her perfume. Letters of heartache; letters of love: all four. His throat tightened; his jaw now tense as his emotions fought to break loose; the desire to have her next to him, to feel her embrace. He unwrapped the plastic covering from his wallet and took her picture out. His want for her pulsated inside him. His heart beat faster; her picture physically stirring him.

"Squad leaders' meeting in thirty minutes. We're headed back to the mountain," the command post messenger yelled into the hooch.

The loud voice jolted the squad leader from his thoughts of her. He brought the picture to his lips, putting it back into his wallet. He wrapped the wallet back into its plastic protection, now safe from water. More commotion on the bridge; word of their new mission was out. He thought of the body in the water: And their next operation to the mountain. He shook his head as if to clear the war from his mind: Only good letters home. He pictured her; her beauty inside and out brought him peace. He started his letter to her: "How's my Angel of Happiness? All is well here…"

CHAPTER 16

Consequence Undetermined

The marine squad leader waited next to the command bunker with his men. He and his squad were choppered in for a special mission and he was anxious to learn what it was. The whistle of mortars pierced the air. The blasts shook the tarmac. The squad leader ordered his squad to encircle the command bunker. They had no designated area to cover. Sirens wailed. Pilots scrambled to their planes. "Incoming" blared over the loud speakers. The pilot of a small scout plane jumped into the cockpit, its engine roared to life. The plane sailed down the runway as if released from a sling-shot. Fifty yards out, the pilot pulled it straight up into the sky, its engine screaming, and then banked north; toward Charlie Ridge: a hunter going to work putting eyes from the air on the enemy mortar teams.

The squad would soon be doing their specialty; seek out, close with, and destroy the enemy. The squad leader entered the command post bunker. "Sir" he greeted his lieutenant, and nodded to his gunny sergeant.

"Grab a coffee Corporal, and pull up a seat." The lieutenant handed him a map. He looked at the red circle between Charlie Ridge and the air base: a kill zone, enemy activity high.

"Tonight you'll be setting up an ambush to stop Charlie." the lieutenant said. The squad leader looked at him.

"A night ambush doesn't make this mission different from others. What does?" he asked.

"Tonight you'll lead a special team. Ten men; seven will be ARVNs, three will be your choice from your team."

The squad leader sipped coffee and stared at the map. They would be in the middle of a VC hornet's nest. What bothered him was the

ARVNs; Army of the Republic of Vietnam forces. A few weeks ago a special team went out; just the ARVNs came back. His marines knew and trusted each other with their lives. He didn't know or trust the ARVNs, some of them worked both sides of battle. He didn't like the three–seven balance. He felt a familiar inner warning: God's whisper.

"I would rather take seven of my men and three ARVNs," he said.

"You don't have that option," the lieutenant replied.

"After what happened to the other special team?" the squad leader asked.

"We don't know what happened out there, corporal," the Gunny said.

"It's not the first time," the squad leader stated. He thought of his men, all under twenty years old, like him. He chose his words. "Sir, our men deserve a better answer."

"I know, but it's the only one we've got," the lieutenant said.

The squad leader's gut tightened. "Sir, I respectfully decline the order as given. There are too many unanswered variables."

Disbelief flashed across the lieutenant's face. "Do you know you can be shot for disobeying an order in battle?"

"Sir, I will not knowingly let my men be ambushed," he said. He stood up.

"You are dismissed, corporal." the lieutenant said.

The squad leader walked back to his men. He respected the lieutenant and the gunny. The lieutenant's words drained his spirit. "Lord, it's in your hands," he whispered. He entered the hooch and sat on a cot. He had never challenged an order. But he didn't regret his action, just wished he had not been put into that position. His men gathered around him.

"What's happ'ning?" his radioman asked.

"Ambush by the ridge," he said, referring to the area of the red circle. "Not sure of the itinerary yet," the leader replied. "The lieutenant and gunny are still working on it." The gunny walked in.

"You'll need this," the gunny said. He handed him the map. "There's been a change. Headquarters doesn't feel ready to send ARVNs out with you—yet. They want answers to the last incident. Get your men saddled up. You're moving out at 1900 hours; de-briefing at 0900 hours in the morning, corporal."

There was no anger, no animosity—all three of them doing their job the best they could. He still wasn't sure of the consequences of his challenge. But his heart felt good.

CHAPTER 17

Jungle Predator

The twelve-man marine squad pushed through the jungle, part of a search-and-destroy mission hunting for a VC unit and their camp. They were the hunters that could become the hunted in an instant. Nerves had been strained for hours. Morning fog cloud thick, humidity you pushed through. The silence screamed. The squad leader felt the chill on the back of his neck. God's whisper. He had felt it before. Never wrong. Something watched them.

He dropped on one knee, arm raised with closed fist, the signal for imminent danger. The marines moved as shadows, blending into the jungle. Something stirred in the jungle canopy. The branches moved: no breeze.

"Above us," he yelled.

A shadow fell toward them. The marines opened fire. It fell on the radioman, slamming them both to the jungle floor; a huge snake.

"Hold your fire," the squad leader ordered.

"What the…" the radioman shouted.

"Maybe python, maybe boa, maybe something else; who knows what lives in this place," the squad leader said.

Bullets had ripped into the great snake. It still moved, twisting and thrashing. Seven man-steps long and so thick you couldn't reach your fingers of both hands around it. The radioman raised his rifle to shoot the beast.

"Let it live," the squad leader said.

"Man, it tried to eat me," the radioman replied.

"Or maybe it fell off a branch trying to get away from your ugly ass," the squad leader said. I don't like 'em. They're hard to kill. This one's not dying, just hurt'en a little." The snake slid between the marines without aggression and made its way into the brush, disappearing without a sound.

He scanned the jungle. "Snakes don't fall unless they're spooked. He came through us to get away. Whatever bothered him came from the west of us." He pointed to the opposite direction the snake had taken.

"What makes you think that?" the radioman asked. He adjusted the radio pack on his back. The snake had jostled the straps when it hit.

"I've hunted since I was nine. Hunted animals act on instinct to stay alive. The snake was more afraid of something over there than us. Stay sharp. Close up the ranks: Whisper distance," the squad leader ordered.

The lieutenant and the other two squads were east of them, moving up the mountain. He motioned the radioman to him.

"Update the lieutenant on our position," he said to the radioman.

"Where the hell are we?" the radioman asked, pretending ignorance.

"'Nam," the squad leader joked. He felt the squad's tension ease. He took the radio handset to report to the lieutenant.

Their orders were the same; continue up the ridge. The other squads had not seen camps or enemy. He signaled his point man to move out. They worked their way forward for two hours. He still felt watched. He stopped the squad and waited in silence. The fog that had blocked the sight of enemy movement earlier now had lifted. The reek of burnt wood wafted through the trees.

"Stop and drop," he whispered to the rifleman in front of him. He put his palm facing the ground and lowered his hand, then sunk to the earth; the signal for hasty ambush. The squad dropped to the jungle floor. Nothing moved. No sounds. The squad leader pointed to the point man and then tapped himself on the chest, the signal to follow him. "We'll recon ahead. It could be the camp," he whispered.

He crept forward; the point man behind. They were a stone's throw ahead of the squad. He scanned the trail in front. A mound of fresh raised dirt went from the trail to a log wedged in a tree, a car's length from them. Sharpened bamboo stakes stuck out; a thin rope ran up to branches: A punji swing booby trap.

He motioned his point man back. A bamboo pole propped against the punji log held it in place. He could see a few feet of the bamboo then it went into the ground. The fresh dirt covered the pole. It was the trigger. When bumped, the log would swing toward the trail. He inched backward. A blur caught his glance: movement in the brush behind the punji log; then gone. He thumbed his rifle to full auto. Two images darted from behind the log: VC. He opened fire at them. Enemy fire came from his west and from the front. His squad opened fire. Ambush! The VC hidden in the brush had waited for them.

"Guns up," he shouted. The machine-gun team came in behind him. "Cut 'em down," he yelled, pointing to the muzzle flashes in the brush. "Third team, cover our back," he ordered. The firefight lasted just minutes. The VC moved back further into the jungle; their return fire sporadic.

"They're running," the radioman yelled. He stood up and stepped off the trail. The squad leader grabbed his shirt and yanked him back.

"Hold your positions. No one moves off the trail," the squad leader ordered. He was uneasy. The VC broke off too fast. They wanted to be chased. He signaled the blooper man up. His M-79 weapon used an explosive shell the size of a lemon. Accurate: and deadly.

"Take out the swing," the squad leader ordered. He pointed to the booby trap. The marine raised his weapon and fired. The punji swing shattered into pieces. The marines fell back to the ground. Crashing noises came from where the VC had been. A scream pierced the jungle brush. Then silence. The marines readied for another assault. The squad leader looked into the jungle at their side. A second punji trap now swung between two trees; either hooked to the first trap or the blast had triggered it. The enemy had vanished. Smoke came from the direction the VC ran.

"Cut a bamboo pole for probing," the squad leader ordered his men. They had to go toward the scent of the burning wood. That meant leaving the trail; more booby traps. He reported to the lieutenant of their enemy contact.

"1st and 3rd Squads are clear of your grid. It will take two hours to get there. Air support is ready; at your call," the lieutenant said.

"We'll move ahead," the squad leader said.

"Take it slow," he ordered his point man. They moved past the second punji swing. A bloodied piece of shirt dangled on one of its sharpened teeth; the reason for the VC scream. They stalked the VC and burnt wood scent for a hundred yards, probing for traps as they went. The smell of burnt wood so strong in his mouth, the squad leader could taste it. They were closing in on a fire pit. The point man stopped and dropped to one knee. The squad leader moved up to him. They had breached the exterior of the VC camp.

No enemy movement. The squad leader brought up his arms out-stretched, waist high, and moved them inward toward the camp. The squad moved up on both sides of him, a frontal assault position; the machine-gun team at the center. All would have a clear field of fire at the enemy. They swept into the camp. Six fire pits dug into the ground;

each about the size of a trash can lid; all extinguished with dirt; three still warm and smoking. A dozen brush lean-to for shelter. No huts. They moved through the camp. It could shelter forty to sixty VC: a staging area for enemy movement, now empty. He marked the coordinates on his map and reported to the lieutenant. Their orders; sweep the camp for intel then head to their extraction point.

The squad leader stopped at a fire pit. Next to it a rope clothes line was strung between two moss-covered trees. A frayed shirt hung on it. Next to the shirt three snakeskins draped over the line, stripped of meat, the skins the same size and color of the snake that had dropped on the squad.

"Do you think the snake this morning thought he was being hunted?" the radioman asked. He took his knife and cut the line. The shirt and skins fell onto the covered hot coals and burst into flames; the smell of burning cloth and snakeskin permeated the air.

The squad leader thought of the snake. The VC close enough to scare it: close enough to ambush the marines. That's why he had felt watched. The snake disrupted the VC ambush. He shook off the chill that went through him.

"Everything in this place becomes hunted sooner or later. War is the ultimate predator," the squad leader whispered.

The Mountain Ledge

The squad leader moved the twelve-man squad out of the abandoned VC camp, the enemy now rousted by the marine drive up the mountainside. The size of the camp suggested fifty to sixty VC. "Advance to new coordinates," the orders passed to him from his lieutenant.

"Keep sharp guys, we still don't know where they are," he said to the squad.

They were coming to a sparsely covered ridge line, part of a bare ledge. At the far side of the ledge, a stone's throw away, waist-high brush grew with small thick trees, their growth stunted by the rock that formed the ledges. He signaled for the squad to stop. He felt uneasy; the open ground ahead gave no chance for cover; the thick shrubs gave the enemy a place to hide in wait for the squad, a prime place for an enemy ambush. He went up to his point man.

"See anything yet?" he asked him.

"No. I think they are way ahead of us."

"Maybe, but I wish I felt as sure." the squad leader said. "Cover me. I'm going for a look-see over to the edge of the ledge." He walked toward the ledge, the squad now in defense position, every other man facing opposite directions, ready for an assault from any side.

He had hunted deer in the mountains back home. At times he would find a deer yard, a place where a dozen or more deer stayed for safety. Most times, the deer would run and the hunter would chase after; but sometimes, either out of fear of the hunter or just wise enough to wait and determine which way to escape, they ran just a short distance, then lay down behind a log, or stood motionless among low-hanging tree branches, their image shielded from even the most skilled hunter's sight.

The first time his father had taken him to the hunting camp he was twelve. He had sat on the edge of his cot as his dad and five other men talked at the table as they played cards. He wiped his rifle with a dry cloth, and listened intently to them speak. He had pictured himself there with his dad since he was nine. His dad would take him or one of his four brothers on a Saturday afternoon hunt for squirrel or partridges. His sister was too young to go. He wasn't allowed to carry a rifle then. It had been like a rite of passage when he was at deer camp, with his own borrowed rifle laid across his lap. He felt pride within him as the men listened to his dad go over the hunting plan for the morning.

He and his dad left camp at early dawn; his dad leading the way. They had gone only a short distance, maybe two hundred yards up an old logging road, when his dad signaled with his open hand shoulder high; stop; don't move. He stopped, looking for the reason. To their right, he saw half a dozen of the white tails of deer as they ran from them. Next to a log stood a deer; a doe. They would only shoot buck. They watched maybe two minutes. He was impatient; he wanted to chase down the deer that he had seen.

He shuffled his feet; his world exploded into action. A huge buck burst up from behind the log, his antlers glistened in the morning light.

It ran hard, its belly almost touching the ground; the smallest target he could be; the buck now a blur to him. It ran back in the direction of the camp. Youth and inexperience froze him with surprise. He lifted his rifle but too late. In a matter of seconds, the buck disappeared deeper into the woods. He was between the deer and his dad. His dad couldn't shoot. His dad walked up to him and put his hand on his shoulder.

"Don't feel bad," he said. "The buck was smart waiting us out, hoping we would pass. He figured his best chance was to run back that way; he was right. The lesson from this; never underestimate what you're hunting," he said

The squad leader had never forgotten that lesson. He moved his thumb to the full-auto lever and thumb-flicked his rifle to full auto mode. He went to the edge; his breathing shallow, muscles taut. He peered over the edge. "VC," he shouted to the squad. A VC lay in a crevice just below the top edge of the ledge, just a few feet away. The VC jumped up and faced the marine, his hands at his sides; his rifle in one hand; pointed toward the ground. The squad leader saw the fear in his face; the hesitation it created.

The squad leader had his rifle aimed at the VC's chest.

"Chieu Hoi, Chieu Hoi," the squad leader yelled to him: words for the VC to surrender. The VC acted stunned. "Chieu hoi," he yelled again. The VC laid his rifle down on top of the ledge and stepped to the top.

"My God, just a kid," the squad leader said. The VC looked about the same age as the squad leader's younger twin brothers, maybe thirteen or fourteen. Screams in Vietnamese came from the brush. The young VC turned toward the sound. The voice screamed again at him. He reached to pick up his rifle.

"No, don't, don't" the squad leader yelled. Rifle fire came from the brush. He dove between two rock outcrops. The squad returned fire; the machine-gun team sprayed into the brush and trees. The VC grabbed up his rifle and began shooting. The squad leader fired a burst on auto into the tree line. He lifted his rifle over the rock, keeping his head down, firing wild bursts toward where the VC had been. He wasn't sure where he was anymore.

The enemy assault stopped. The marines waited, not knowing the enemy's numbers or positions. The squad leader thought of the VC camp that may have held sixty or more enemy. Five minutes; then ten minutes: an eternity to wait for the unknown; the ledges now deathly quiet.

He stood and saw the fallen VC at the edge of the ledge. He signaled the squad to sweep the area. They needed to make sure the enemy had all been taken out. He stopped by the fallen VC and crouched down on one knee, still looking all around for enemy. He checked him to see if he was breathing: nothing. He wasn't sure if he or the squad's return fire had stopped him. He had not wanted it this way; he wanted to have him surrender. The enemy lay there; a child just becoming a man; or a man who still wanted to be a child.

"Frigging war," the squad leader whispered. Sadness overwhelmed him. He wiped the enemy's face with his towel. He wished he knew what the enemy in the brush had yelled. If it wasn't for that, the young VC would be alive now.

"Just one in the brush: dead now. You okay?" the radioman asked him. Sweat ran down his forehead; a tell-tale sign of the tenseness of the firefight.

"What's okay in war," the squad leader replied. It wasn't a question, just a statement. He stood up, slung his towel around his neck. None in the squad had been hit. "Get the lieutenant on the horn," he said to the radioman. The lieutenant needed to know their status and situation.

The squad leader felt drained after giving his report. "Intel chopper coming for the two KIAs: Extraction choppers coming for us. Secure the perimeter," he ordered the squad. He went to the edge of the ledge and sat down. He looked down the shallow valley; now silent; serene. He took his canteen and poured water onto his towel, attempting to wash the blood away. He scrubbed it hard against the ledge; the life's blood of youth now seeping into the rocks' crevices. He heard the echo of the choppers coming up the valley. He stood and looked over at the youth lying on the barren stone. He thought again of his younger brothers, probably out snowmobiling on the Hill, a favorite spot, just a few miles from home. Emotion overcame him. He rubbed the towel across his face, feeling its wet coolness, but still tainted with the smell of blood. The towel could be washed; the memory of this ledge he was not sure: only time would tell.

CHAPTER 18

Seek and Hide and Find

The twelve-man marine squad moved toward the tree line, the mid-morning sun at their back. VC ran into the trees ahead of them. The enemy was on the run. The squad was part of a company-sized sweep and was joined with a regiment of ROK marines. They moved ahead for an hour, staying in contact with the rest of their platoon, not wanting to get ahead or behind of the marine sweep. They reached the backside of the trees. The terrain slopped down into a small valley, blanketed with yellowed, dying, man-high elephant grass.

The squad leader saw trails of grass flattened. The hair on the back of his neck prickled. He moved his squad down the slope into the valley. He tried to radio his lieutenant. They couldn't make contact with anyone. They were on their own. He heard voices ahead of them, and motioned his squad to stop and drop. The voices talked fast and excited; in Vietnamese. They could hear but not see them. He inched forward until he found a part in the grass. They had almost walked onto another trail. This one led toward the river. He moved closer. He saw a force of VC round a bend in the trail, then out of sight. He guessed over thirty. They had come from the ridge above them and were trying to elude the marine sweep. He realized his squad was ahead of the other marine force. He moved back to his men and tried to make radio contact with their platoon: Nothing. The men looked at him, waiting for his command to engage the VC. He shook his head. They were outnumbered, no radio contact, and didn't know the exact location of the rest of the platoon. They worked their way up to the tree line on the other side. There they made radio contact with their lieutenant. Parts of a VC regiment were in front of them and had been pushed to the river. Command base called in an air strike on the enemy force.

He saw the two F-4 Phantom jets streak down out of the sky and flash past them, before he heard their thunderous scream. Their surface-to-ground rockets hit less than five hundred yards in front of the marines, tearing into the VC force. The Phantom jets circled back, doing a roll-over salute to the marines and then headed straight up into the sky, the rest of their payload to be delivered to their primary target elsewhere.

"Move up!" the lieutenant ordered over the radio. The squad leader looked at his men. Young faces trained on him waited for the order.

"Move out," he commanded and moved forward to engage the enemy.

CHAPTER 19

Unexpected Visitor

Beads of red-stained sweat moved down the squad leader's bare chest and midriff. It soaked into the beltline of his green jungle fatigues. He sat on his cot. His flak jacket and bandoliers of ammo placed at the bottom: his rifle next to the pillow; the clip inserted partway, just a slap from being locked and loaded. He was silent. He rubbed his eyes; squelching the tears and erasing any emotions. Head resting in the palms of his hands, eyes closed; his body grew taut as he thought of the four marines.

A man stepped into the doorway of the hooch.

"Heard you've been giving the VC hell," he said.

"Hell is all around us," the squad leader replied. He looked toward the man, saw the marine sergeant chevron on his sleeve, but did not recognize him. The man's voice seemed vaguely familiar.

"Heard you guys have been on an op for a few weeks, got a couple hundred of 'em," the marine in the doorway said.

"Four," the squad leader said.

"What do you mean; four?"

"The only number I count. The number of men we lost on the mission."

The marine in the doorway stepped into the hooch. "I didn't know. I'm sorry. Are you okay?"

The squad leader stared at the man but the front of his bush hat was pulled down and covered part of his face. The man had a full mustache.

He still did not know who he was or why he was here; or why he showed such concern.

"You don't remember me do you?" the other marine asked. "I'll show you who I was with two weeks ago." He walked to the cot and took a picture from his shirt. He showed it to the squad leader. It was the squad leader's Love.

"You lying piece of shit," the squad leader bellowed and lunged up from the cot at him, grabbing him by his throat. "Where did you get her picture?"

"I'm her brother, I'm her brother," the other marine yelled out. The squad leader released him, and backed away.

"God, you got jungle in you," the other marine said.

"It keeps me alive," the squad leader replied and extended his arm in friendship.

He had met her brother just once. Her brother was home on leave, clean shaven and in regular clothes. He would soon head back for his second tour in-country, a sergeant in charge of a transport convoy unit. They had gone to the Polka-Dot, a local all-night diner, for coffee. The squad leader was not in the Marines then. He was working construction.

"What are your intentions with my sister?" her brother had asked.

"That's between us and none of your business." he had answered. The coffee was hot; the atmosphere was cold, for a few moments. They respected each other and left it that way. Now he was here in the squad leader's hooch.

"How did you find me?" the squad leader asked.

"I've been trying to catch up with you, but every time I cross paths with your unit, you're in the Bush. God, you're all slashed to shit."

The squad leader looked at his bloodied hands and arms.

"Don't tell her. It's my new look. How is she?" the squad leader asked. His heart jumped. His voice cracked.

Emotions ran strong as they talked about her; and families and home: And her.

The marine's Love, writing to him from half a world away.

Twenty minutes. That's all the time they had: They extended their hand; gripping each other's forearm; a warrior's handshake. Her brother turned to leave.

"Be good, be careful. May the good Lord take a liking to ya, but not too soon." he said; a saying passed down from his Love's father at every goodbye.

Neither one knew when; or if, they would see the other alive again.

CHAPTER 20

The Devil's Playground

Rain beat down on the canvas hooch. Hard rain; all day, every day and all night, every night; monsoon season. The squad leader lay on his cot, back from a night action two hours ago as dawn broke without the sun. He closed his eyes, inhaling the fragrance that drifted up to him: Wing Song: Hers; with its memories; her arms around his neck; her hair across his face. He held her open letter, savoring the moment. "God, please bring me back to her," he whispered.

Shouting jarred him to his feet. He tucked the letter into his wallet, grabbed his rifle and flak jacket and ran out of his hooch. Angry voices in the compound. A marine lay on the ground. Blood flowed from above his eye, mixing into the red mud of Vietnam. Four marines threw stones at him. Their bush hats and green T-shirts were streaked with mud as if they had been fighting. The squad leader ran and got him to his feet. He looked for help. Where the hell is everybody? Stones struck against them as he held the other marine up. No one came out from their hooches. It wasn't because of the downpour. He knew the truth. The marine that was hurt was white. The stone throwers were black. Nobody wanted to get involved. It was bullshit.

He moved them forward. His stride kept an even pace across the base compound, his body blocking most of the stones from hitting the other marine. He raised his open palm high in the air for the stone throwers to stop. "You start this?" he asked the bleeding marine. He didn't know if he had antagonized them, but knew he had before. Damn the black–white hate shit. He didn't understand why the hate was there. His squad was a mix of race; white, black, brown (Mexican). From all he had experienced, the Corps treated all the same; green. Their marine unit scheduled to go home, was now "stood down." That meant no more operations in the Bush, just local patrols around the command base. Their duties now comprised burning the latrine waste, picking up litter and having drill formations. Damn the formations. Marching, drills, polishing jungle boots, tuck in your shirt, shave: petty crap, but needed when they got stateside. Two weeks ago they had been covering each other's back, now this, restlessness because of boredom. The squad leader thought of words his mother used at times: idle hands make a devil's playground.

"Put the stones down. The enemy is out there," he said. He pointed to the mountains, ominous now; blurred by the downpour.

"We got nothing against you. Just get away from him," the taller attacker yelled, and grabbed for another rock.

"That's not going to happen," the squad leader said.

"Get me out of here," the bleeding marine whispered.

"This ends here and now," the squad leader said. He held him from running. He walked toward the attackers. He didn't know their rank. It didn't matter. They were wrong. "The battalion's going home. Most of us are going back with it. That's a good thing. I can't believe you want brig time when you get back," he said.

"You!" He pointed to the tall attacker. "Take this marine to the corpsmen. You others get back to your hooch. The lieutenant's heard about this by now. You'll be dealing with him." He turned to leave then stopped and faced them. "I remember you from training: same men, same trouble. Better lose your hate before it gets you killed." The tall marine who had thrown stones helped the hurt marine across the compound. The squad leader figured they could mend fences on the way to the corpsman. He left them and walked back to his hooch. He wasn't sure if he was angry at them or mad because not everybody was going back with the battalion. He had not been notified yet. What is: is, he thought. That was his mantra about things in the present. There's nothing he could do about it.

He sat on his cot, grabbed his green towel from his neck and buried his face in its familiar coarse texture. The scent of his sweat, the taste of the mud of Vietnam, and the smell of blood had merged together and formed a fabric of frustration. He wiped his head then threw the towel into the corner of the hooch, as if that in itself would wipe away his memory of war. He lay back on his cot and took her letter from his wallet. Her words spoken to him as if she was sitting on his lap in her upstairs center room. He closed his hand, feeling her hand in his.

"Corporal, report to the lieutenant. Your orders are in," a messenger yelled into the hooch. The squad leader put his lips on the letter, and then put it back in his wallet. He walked into the downpour. Would he be going back to the heaven of her embrace, or a different part of hell? He entered the bunker. His lieutenant and the gunny sergeant sat on ammo boxes. The lieutenant was college, ROTC. The gunny came up through the ranks, both battle-tested combat marines. The lieutenant laid some papers on his box desk, setting a paperweight on them.

"Pull up a seat," he said. He pointed to an ammo box. "What are your thoughts on the incident in the compound?"

"I don't know the baggage those marines carry, but there is no excuse for that kind of action, sir."

"They're all going back to the states. We're sending them back early with the unit. Maybe they'll figure it out there," the lieutenant said. "We all want to go home early, but the end result is a third of us won't. You'll be coming with the gunny and I, and a few others. We'll be forming with another Rapid Assault Force." The lieutenant handed him the orders. He thought about the men getting to go home. He took a breath and exhaled.

"Four days and we'll be in another part of hell together, sir."

"We know you'll be packing light," the gunny said.

The squad leader knew his meaning; no hateful baggage. He shook the gunny's hand, saluted his lieutenant and left the bunker. He went back to his hooch. He threw his helmet on his cot and picked up his tin cup of black coffee; half gone and cold. He finished it, dumped in some water from his canteen, sloshed it around then swallowed it. He thought of the paper on the lieutenant's desk. Words the lieutenant had written in red, the chosen few. Under that were the squad leader's name and then a dozen or so more. A white rectangular paperweight sat on the top edge of the paper. Etched in bronze in its center were the words: Matthew 5:9. He knew part of that verse: Blessed are the Peacemakers. He squared his shoulders, the unseen weight lifted.

Protectors and Protesters

The monsoon rain dimmed mid-afternoon to twilight. The squad leader moved his twelve-man squad through the vill; the marines at high alert. They had worked up the mountain for hours, the torrential rain not allowing choppers to fly. This was a friendly vill: attacked a day and a half ago by VC. The villagers were farmers, unarmed. Lucky ones had run and hid. A dozen lay motionless on the ground where they had fallen, their lives taken.

The squad leader came to a child sitting in red mud; her black hair matted; her dark eyes bloodshot; shivering as the deluge of the monsoon assaulted her. She shook the battered body of an old man. Blood no longer flowed from the wound in his chest. His right hand still clenched a garden hoe with blood on the end; evidence of a battle lost. She was worn out from trying to awaken him: Four, maybe five years old; too young to comprehend death. Or the shock of death too much for her to bear. She grabbed the squad leader's leg. A tremor went through his body.

He had learned to mentally distance himself from death; locking down his feelings. Her tiny hand gripped his leg. It jarred his being and unlocked the door to his emotions. He held back tears as he bent down and took her hand from his leg. He needed to check the vill for enemy. She spoke to him, her voice weak from crying. The monsoon stole her words.

"Corpsman up," he yelled. The corpsman spoke Vietnamese; some.

The corpsman checked the old man and stood up. His bandage pack swung at his hip, open but still full. The dead didn't need bandages. The girl cradled the old man's face in her lap, keeping it above the mud.

How do I tell her he's gone?" he asked the squad leader.

"You don't." The squad was exhausted from their non-stop push to get here; skin peeled from water-soaked hands that had grabbed trees and rocks to pull them up the mountainside. He had felt that dread;

the apprehension of what they would find when they reached the vill. The report of the attack had come so late. A silent scream grew inside him. They could not be everywhere at once. "You tell her that she did good. You tell her that she kept him alive. You tell her that we'll take him now and try to make him better. Find a villager to take care of her."

The VC would plunder the vill on their way back, maybe in a couple days. The marines would be here when they came. There were two more marine squads on the mountain; below the vill attempting to cut off the VC from going down into the valley. "Set up perimeter defenses," the squad leader said. They would stay until choppers could fly the villagers out. Two days or ten; it didn't matter. His mission directive: protect the villagers until they could be relocated.

A week later the squad leader sat on his heels in a forward base bunker. The rest of the squad had dispersed to take advantage of a few hours' downtime. He reached into his fatigue pocket and pulled out his lighter; words engraved into the side. He lit a nickel-size chunk of C-4 explosive and warmed the beef and rocks c-rat meal over the scorching flame. "Rocks seem a funny name for potatoes; unless you taste one from c-rations," he said aloud, not expecting a response. The rain pelted down outside the open entryway, the dirt in the compound ankle-deep mud. He couldn't remember if this was dinner or supper: didn't matter what time of day. He wasn't sure if he'd had breakfast. Now four o'clock by his watch. He had no set time to eat any more; he ate when he was hungry; sometimes not at all; depending on the mission.

As he ate, his eyes locked onto a piece of paper; wrappings from someone's care package; a couple of weeks old. He picked it up. The smell of old damp paper permeated into his senses. Its headline bold letters: **GET US OUT OF VIETNAM—IT'S NOT OUR WAR.** He had never known hate until a few months ago: he had learned to hate what the enemy did to get their way. He didn't hate the protesters. He just hated the way some tried to take a person's values and dignity away: the same way as the enemy; by intimidation and force. His captain had kicked three news reporters out of his hooch. They wanted to stage a false assault through a vill so they could get action shots of a marine sweep.

A week ago he had been on the mountain. The villagers there had paid an unimaginable price for just wanting to raise their children, to grow their crops, to live their life; in peace. But they didn't have anybody there in time to fight for them…

The day he had turned twelve he was chopping firewood on the porch for the cook stove and his mother had come out with two cups of hot tea; he could tell she had been crying. She did sometimes when she thought about her family in Austria. They sat on two of the chopping blocks and put one in front of them; a makeshift table. She took the tea bag strings and moved the bags up and down in the green Melmac cups; her eyes distant. It was July. Sweat ran down his face; but he drank the hot tea anyway. The aroma of orange and spice mixed with the smell of the split maple logs.

They talked about the woodpile; they talked about school; they talked about friends. She was quiet for a moment. Then she started to talk about her family in Austria. She had not seen them in over fourteen years. She received a letter or two a year, one coming around Christmas time. She had gotten a letter from her mother that morning. She pulled it out of the pocket of her beige-colored apron with the red flowers embroidered across the front. The envelope was already torn open; he didn't know how many times she had read it earlier. She read aloud, and cried. He listened; as much as a twelve-year-old could. When she had finished, she slowly folded it and put it back into her apron.

She and her family had fled the Nazis in World War II: hiding by day, moving by night. Her country's hope was dim; until the Americans came to help. That's how she had met, and then married his dad. She had gotten her citizenship when he was seven or eight years old. They'd had a family gathering that day to celebrate. His uncle had asked her how it felt to be free in America.

"No one is truly free until everyone is free," she had said.

The squad leader dropped the paper into the fire and pictured the little girl on the mountain; the old man who had fought and died. He gripped his lighter in his pocket, his fingers slid across the words now etched in his mind: "For those who have fought for it, freedom has a taste the protected will never know."

CHAPTER 21

The Face of the Enemy

The heat was stifling. No breeze. Beads of sweat formed on the squad leader's lean, muscular body. His sun-bronzed chest and weathered flak jacket draped with bandoliers of ammo rose and fell in tempo with every breath. His steel helmet hung heavy in his left hand. His rifle slung "at the ready," his right hand cradled the trigger; his face calm as he looked at the picturesque scene in front of him.

Green, lush rice paddies laid out in square patterns fenced in by earthen dikes, a few elderly mama-sons, and pop-pa-sons hoed the rice, standing in the water with their pant legs rolled up to their knees. A massive water buffalo stood at the edge of the paddy and stared at him. He saw three baby-sons playing in the door opening of their grass hooch. The marine's face and the village's peaceful beauty hid the horrors of war that each had experienced.

This was a peaceful vill. They started to move through it. One of his squad reached up to pick a green banana from its lofty perch. The squad leader grabbed his wrist. They would take nothing without asking. He saw the villagers coming from the backside of the hooches. The village elder had his family with him, a rare show of friendship. He handed the squad leader a drink. Looking into the villager's eyes searching for treachery, seeing only gratitude and kindness, he took the drink, scanning their surroundings as his squad drank.

There was a cook fire, smoke spiraling upwards, a man standing next to it. Something was different about this villager. Noticing a fresh cut down the side of the man's face, he pointed to it and the man replied in halting English that he had fought VC a few nights ago. The squad leader's mind flashed back two days to a firefight his squad was in. It had not been far from this vill. There was something in the villager's eyes that said it was the truth but more was shielded. The squad finished their drinks and soon left the vill, leaving as quietly as they came.

He received orders to set up a night act (ambush) on the north side of the vill; 1st Squad would set up on the west side. His squad had only seven men; short five marines of a full twelve-man squad. They moved through the night, and settled into their position; claymore mines were set out, each man in his position watching for the enemy. The squad

leader mentally checked everything; the field of fire, the claymore's blast angle, had the men check their ammo. He felt uneasy; that this night would not be calm.

Just after midnight he heard the whisper on their prc-25 radio: 1st squad reports an enemy force has moved very close to their location and has started to dig up a weapons cache. They requested support. Their squad had only seven men. They were outnumbered by the VC.

The squad leader gave the command to saddle up. He knew the risk they would be taking; moving fast through the darkness; the enemy close. But his squad were the only friendlies close enough to get there in time. The radioman ran next to the squad leader, whispering into the handset to the other squad that they were coming. They were almost there. The radioman signaled with rapid clicking of his handset and they closed in behind the other squad.

The squad leader watched the enemy dig at their weapons cache, counting eighteen VC, around sixty to seventy yards in front of them, between the marines and the edge of the vill. He called command base for illumination mortar rounds at their coordinates. The incoming mortar whistled then burst, turning the night into brilliant day; the signal for the marines to open fire on the enemy force.

The VC were overwhelmed by the surprise onslaught; in chaos. Some stood there confused and returned fire, not seeking any defensive stance or position, frozen with fear. Others scrambled to hide behind ponchos hanging on bushes, firing on the marines. It was like they were playing hide and seek thinking that if they covered their eyes, they could not be seen.

Four VC ran to the side along the edge of the vill and out of sight. The squad leader had two of his men cover their flanks in case the VC attacked from there. Three of the VC jumped into the weapons cache hole and fired on the marines. The marine 2nd Squad fired on them until there was no more return fire from them. The squads started taking fire from their flank, where the four VC had run. The marines covering their flank were ready and returned fire, taking them down. The leader looked across the field of fire, mentally noting the enemy down, calculating the number of enemy still able to fight. Five or six were still out there somewhere.

He turned to the rear, an inner instinct guiding him. He reached to change clips. A VC came over the dike and he rose to meet him. He didn't have time to put in a fresh clip. The enemy's rifle pointed to his chest. Time stopped. He grabbed at the rifle, not wanting death to win here. The VC pulled the trigger. Everything was quiet: there was no pain: no sting of death: just the clear click of an empty chamber.

He saw the VC's face; only a rifle length away. The scar: it was the man that he had seen at the vill. The VC thrust his bayonet at him, slicing the outside of his right arm as he deflected it. The will to live surged through him. He thrust the barrel of his rifle through the neck of the demon before him. In the light of the illumination he saw the disbelief in his enemy's face. There was no scream, only silence, as life left his body.

Two more VC came over the dike, with more silhouettes behind them. He pulled out another clip, slammed it home, and fired it at the VC still coming. He kept firing and reloading. His arms were tired, so tired. Every time he slammed in another clip, his rifle barrel fell toward the ground. It seemed so heavy. Maybe this was how death felt. Something inside him would not accept it. He saw his men beside him, each in their own struggle to live. This would not be their night to die. The return fire was getting quieter; the muzzle flashes were further away. The VC were done.

He swung his rifle across the field of fire. The light of the fresh illumination mortars caught something in front of him. The reality of what had just happened hit him. On the end of his rifle barrel was the lifeless body of the enemy, still impaled. He lowered the rifle to the ground and gently pulled it free. The face of death had come close this night.

Crucibles and Commendations

The squad leader drew his Ka-Bar from its sheath: its handle a familiar feeling in the palm of his hand. His eyes never left his enemy target, fifteen feet away, moving silently between two wooden stakes. He raised the knife in one fluid motion, and threw toward the target, as if a baseball thrown to home plate. The knife struck the enemy between his beltline and ribcage, spinning him around in a circle; the thud of the hit drifting back to the squad.

Voices rose behind him. The squad leader ran to the target, a cardboard cutout and withdrew the knife. He turned to face the voices; his squad. He watched the face of the newbie; the newest marine to the squad. It was his birthday; just turned eighteen: The knife-throwing part of the "games" at this birthday party for him. He put his knife back into its sheath. His face showed no emotion as his thoughts raced to birthday parties back home. Those were happy times. Not like here. Games at home were for fun. Here, games honed skillsets that he prayed they would never need.

He walked back to the squad, grabbed his can of beer he had set on the empty ammo box; their makeshift table. He laid a dollar bill in its place: not for the beer, but because his knife throw didn't beat one other.

"Nice try," the winning marine said.

Being second was not a bad thing; the marine who won was a champion knife thrower back at his home. Most of his downtime from missions would find him practicing.

"Time for pillow fights," the radioman shouted.

"I'll pass for now," the squad leader said. He smiled. Pillow fights: a friendly name for half-filled sandbags. The players would each hold onto opposite ends of a towel and not let go, swinging a half-filled sand bag at the other. Whoever got knocked down first lost. He moved to the side and set cross-legged on the ground, the newbie joining him. The squad leader looked at him. The newbie had been doing well; a fast learner. The squad leader would be going on a two-man recon mission in a few days. He was going to bring the newbie; but not told him yet. He would tell him that day; not wanting him to get anxious. The birthday celebration would be over soon. It had been a downtime for the squad today; come morning light; they were being inserted onto Charlie Ridge for a search-and-destroy mission. The squad leader toasted the newbie's birthday, they drank the cheer: the party now over.

"Check your gear, get some sleep; write home; we lift off at pre-dawn," he said, and left for his hooch. He needed to write his Love. He needed to feel her quiet gentleness around him. When he wrote her, or read her letters, he felt her encompass him; driving out the badness in the world; and in his thoughts.

He glanced up to the sky checking for storm clouds. He hated the rain; he hated the heat; he hated the war; but the Vietnamese people needed their help. Thoughts came back at him; mental picture of ambushes, firefights, the faces of the enemy as they lay on the red earth, faces of villagers; women and children, walking as if in a trance after a VC attack, looking for loved ones. His jaw tightened. All these things: the crucibles of war.

He entered his hooch, sat on his cot to write his letter to her. He paused, trying to clear his mind; he wrote only good letters home. When does the pendulum of war swing back? He knew ordeals of war he and the squad had been through. The enemy had drawn blood on him in that firefight the first night he was in-country, the AK round hitting his arm; just a flesh wound. He had covered it up; told no one. His promise to her: I won't get hurt, I'll be back: we will spend the rest of our lives together. His squad leader saw the wound the next morning as they left their ambush site. He had pulled him aside and checked it.

"I'll need to report this," he said.

"No. No one needs to know, it's okay. I don't want her to worry," he had told him.

"No report, no record," his squad leader told him.

"My siblings drew more blood than this from me when we played at home. No one needs to know." he had said.

"Your call, keep it washed out," his squad leader said, and it was never mentioned again. A few months ago, they had made contact on a night ambush with a VC courier element carrying intelligence papers. The VC force outnumbered them three-to-one, but they stopped them and captured all the intel papers. The next day the lieutenant said they had been all been put up for the Marine Commendation Medal; with Valor. They gave them a three-day in-country R & R at M.A.G.16; their squad leader spent a week in Bangkok with a four-star general. That was two or three months ago, still no word on the medal. It didn't really matter to him. A few days ago they passed through a friendly vill. The children watched from a distance, but he could see their smiles. They were glad to see the marines; it meant they were safe that night. Maybe that was the pendulum of war swinging back he thought. Crucibles will always be in war; commendations can never be counted on: but the children's smiles stayed with him.

He started his letter to Her… "How's my angel of happiness today? All is well here…"

CHAPTER 22

Bob Hope Show

The chopper lifted the twelve-man marine squad into the sky. Their bush op cut short. The squad leader stood by the window as the thick jungle passed underneath. The VC they hunted the last two days were in there; close. But the squad was now being extracted. Rumor had it they were being pulled from the op to be security for a Bob Hope show coming to Da Nang. "Bob Hope and girls," the men shouted. The squad leader couldn't believe his good luck. Bob Hope was a legend. His mom and dad talked about him. His mother held her hand over her heart pretending a flutter when she watched him on TV. Now he was going to see Bob Hope in person. Maybe he could get a picture with him and then send the film to them to develop; a great surprise.

"Man, I heard Miss America and her entourage were coming too, maybe the Rockettes," the point man said, gyrating his hips. "I hope our spot is next to the stage. I want to reach up and touch those legs. I'm from the Bronx and never saw them at a live show. Boom-boom 'em, that's what I want to do." He tapped his rifle butt onto the chopper deck.

Four days in the Bush, not much sleep, stubble beards, no baths, unless you count bathing in sweat. "They couldn't even tell you were human the way you look; you've been on ops so long you'll be boom-boom 'em tonight in your sleep." the squad leader said. Showers would be their first stop back at the base. Showers and the mess hall: he was eager to clean up, eat and get details of the show. He wasn't sure yet what they would be doing. Word was that the whole platoon, all three squads, would be guarding the show, not getting to watch Bob Hope on stage. If the squad was back stage he could get a bunch of flicks.

They filed off the chopper at command base. He ran to his hooch. He laid his rifle and helmet on his cot, shrugged his pack off his shoulders and let it slip down his arms, landing on the plywood floor. Dropping to his knees he reached under his cot and pulled out his care package from her. He kept his camera there. He wanted to check it. He opened the fold-over cover flaps on the cardboard box, the shipping tape no longer sticky from being opened and closed so many times. He kept the camera on the right-hand side, on the end with the address label. He pulled it out and looked at the flick count; the number in the view window said eighteen. Had he taken eighteen and had six left? Or taken six and had eighteen left. "Man, settle down. It doesn't matter. You know there's film in it," he whispered. He did that more lately; whispering to himself.

He moved aside five packs of Keebler cheese crackers, taking out the sixth, ripped it open with his teeth and shoved a stack of two in his mouth. He kept looking into the box. He was hungry but wanted to make sure he had more film before he cleaned up and went to chow. He found the yellow package of film under the cookies wrapped in wax paper. He grabbed the film and the cookies and pulled them from the box; both a prize. He checked the film; still sealed; twenty-four flicks. The camera and film; ready for the show. He folded the cover flaps back, closing the box, running his hand down the tape to seal it, knowing it no longer would, but did it anyway, then slid it back under the cot.

He jammed a cookie into his mouth, placed the camera and film on the cot, took off his boots, and stripped off his shirt. A leech, longer than his finger, stuck on his rib cage. They had waded across a jungle stream this morning. He had checked himself but missed this one. "Your last meal is over." He pinched, hard; and pulled. The suction broke. Blood ran down his ribcage; a good sign. The opening would clean itself as the blood flowed. He squeezed the leech between his thumb and forefinger until he felt the pop. He walked to the door and threw it into the dust off to the side; onto the common alleyway between the squad hooches. He wiped his hands on his fatigues. He planned to wear them into the shower, cleaning them as well as himself. Instead he unbuttoned them, letting them drop to his feet. He stepped on the trousers leg with one foot, and pulled it off, the same with the other foot. Now naked, he checked for leeches on his skin, found none, wrapped a towel around his waist, grabbed his fatigues and his rifle and headed for the shower. He bit into the last cookie. He may pass up the mess hall; squad leader meeting in an hour. He was in a hurry to find out the squad's placement at the show.

He ran to the mess hall, still twenty minutes until the meeting. Moving past the trays, coming to the coffee, he unclipped his metal cup off his belt loop and filled it, bypassed the sugar and milk, keeping it black. He grabbed three sandwiches; roast beef he hoped. But it was the yellow apple the size of a small melon he spied when he entered the hall that drew him. He grabbed one off the pile and took a quick bite. The taste of its sweet juice reminded him of the apples on the farm where his dad had worked. He'd let him come along sometimes. He was only six or seven years old then, too young to help much but he could eat grain from the cement floor when his dad fed the cattle in the stanchions and he could "cluck" through his teeth as he walked in front of the horses that pulled the hay loader, keeping them settled down so they stayed at a gentle pace. His dad forked the loose hay as it fell from the loader to the wagon. That's when he had that first yellow apple. When they reached a full load of hay his dad had stopped the horses under the apple trees, in the shade.

"You can have an apple but give them each a couple first. They've worked hard," his dad said. The horses had a velvet touch as they took the apple from his hand. Magnificent animals, their heads bigger than he, they'd pulled a hay loader, daisy chained to the hay wagon, as easily as he pulled his red wagon. They stopped a lot under the apple trees that year. He would give the giants their apples, his dad would talk about the land around them. It was the last year his dad worked there.

The squad leader turned back and stuffed two more apples into his shirt, then ran out of the mess hall to the meeting.

He stopped at the steps into his lieutenant's hooch. It was apart from the squad hooches: same size but more private. He reached up and knocked on the open screen door. "Enter," the lieutenant said. He stepped up the three stairs into the hooch. The lieutenant sat on his cot, halfway across the hooch. He wore a green T-shirt: USMC across his chest. He had never seen him in a T-shirt; only full shirts with sleeves rolled up. An old wooden desk was placed near the back. A short stack of papers held down by a paperweight took up most of the desktop. A mismatched chair pushed back from the desk brushed the rear canvas wall. The platoon gunnery sergeant sat on an empty ammo box turned upside down next to a small tarnished metal stand that held the hotplate and coffee fixings. His helmet and flak jacket lay on the floor in front of him, his rifle cradled on top of them. Steam rose from the coffee cup he held as he stirred it with his fingers. Six more empty wooden crates were pushed against the side wall canvas.

"Grab a coffee," said the gunny, pointing to the pot on the hotplate.

The other two squad leaders were not there yet. He looked at his wristwatch.

"You're early," said the gunny. He had seen him do the time check.

"That's a good habit. Get your coffee and find a seat," said the lieutenant and handed him a sheet of paper.

He got the coffee and pulled up a crate next the sergeant. He looked at the paper: Itinerary for the USO show. Bob Hope's name came first, and then Ann Margret, then others, but he stopped reading at Ann Margret.

What a break; Ann Margret on stage. He had watched her sing and dance on TV. Her music had captivated him and he knew the point man would reach for those legs.

"Both Bob Hope and Ann Margret?" he asked.

The lieutenant was somber and passed over the question. "We're part of the security detail. There is intel of a possible enemy thrust from the back side of the pass to target the show with a rocket attack. You have been reassigned to that area to stop it. You won't be at the show."

He knew now why their op had been cut short.

"You're jungle hot, fresh from the Bush. You'll have the edge in a firefight."

The squad leader walked back towards the squad's hooch after the meeting, his coffee cup still half full in his hand. He looked toward the mountain looming in the background. He didn't know the mountain's geological name, but he knew the mountain. They'd had missions there before; a VC haven. The notch in its ominous profile was the pass; the doorway to Da Nang.

Anger, frustration, disappointment; all three surged through his body. He felt the hot coffee before he realized he had crushed the tin cup in his clenched fist. He got closer to his squad's area. He wiped his hand with the bottom of his shirt, then tucked it back in. He kicked dirt back and forth across the splatter on his boots and walked up to the door.

"Anybody got aftershave?" a voice yelled from inside the hooch, the excitement in the words unmistakable. Now he had to tell them that they'd be miles away from Bob Hope and Ann Margret. Instead of wearing aftershave they'd be wearing mud smeared on their faces; instead of setting next to the stage they'd be setting in ambush. But disappointment was no stranger here. You learn to mask your feelings. They'd say little: Maybe a few "f--k its", then they'd get their gear ready for the mission. The mission always comes first.

CHAPTER 23

The Charge of the Christmas Priest

The jungle grass stood motionless; the night air still. The predawn light cast eerie shadows of figures that existed only in eyes that had strained for hours in the darkness watching. The silence was a blessing because of the peace it had brought, but a curse of foreboding for what may be ahead. The marine squad had set in during the night, becoming an unseen part of the land. Their mission: stop any enemy activity. They were at high alert, even now as a new day was awakening. To move too soon would be deadly if they were detected. The leader made a final visual search then signaled to his men to move out. They rose up from the ground, ghostly images, becoming the phantoms of the morning, not breaking the aura of the site.

"Merry Christmas," he whispered to his radioman, and then passed the message down the squad. The two words brought smiles to their face and tempered the tension and strain of the past hours. The message was simple, yet profound, and uplifting. They headed back to the Tower, a bunkered, wooden observation post halfway between two main marine compounds. He was anxious to get back, their night action near completion. Nearing the Tower, they popped a flare to signal their return. The leader expected to be challenged with a call on their radio before they entered the compound. No challenge came. Instinct, God's whisper, triggered his senses, and sent chills up the back of his neck.

"Force entry, go in hot," he commanded. They swarmed the compound, their weapons of war ready to be unleashed on anything that was unusual, out of place, or didn't belong. There were no marines visible.

Inside the compound, the leader silently grouped his men in threes, pointing to different bunkers, in each direction. He took one rifleman and headed to the ladder of the tower. They climbed up the tower: perfect targets. Getting to the top, he dove onto the floor of the Tower; rifle at full ready. He looked across the floor. A man stood at the watch duty post, his glazed eyes stared at the roof as he sang out the words to "One is the Loneliest Number." The leader scanned the room. He saw the enemy lying in a bag on the floor, next to the man. The enemy that had overrun the Tower was dope.

He had never had an incident like this. Disgust made a vile taste in his mouth. He would not, could not tolerate it. The man had proved he could be counted on in a firefight, an asset to their platoon. He was scheduled to rotate back home in a few days. He grabbed the man by the hair and dragged him to the ladder. Telling the rifleman to man the tower for now, he grabbed the bag of dope and headed down the ladder, the wasted marine slung over his shoulder.

His squad had completed the sweep of the compound. No enemy. The other marines on the perimeter wall had seen the flare. Their turn to watch over, they had gone to their bunkers to check their gear for morning patrol. He carried the man to his bunker, and threw him through the opening onto the dirt floor. Anger etched on his face. The man had made a terrible decision, a wrong choice to ease his loneliness and sorrows. It could cost him. The leader shrugged off the anger. What is, is; only what is ahead can be changed he thought to himself.

He headed across the compound, but paused next to a tall, skinny tree. He had bartered it from a village their patrol had gone through, for a dozen chocolate paddy bars. He had saved them for weeks from his meal rations. He smiled when the men asked if he was losing his mind, not knowing why he wanted a tree. This was the first Christmas away from home for most of them, as it was his, and he sensed a sadness none of them would admit.

"This is our Christmas tree," he said. Smiles on their faces and jibber-jabber ideas for decorations filled the journey from the vill back to the tower, these man-boys; eighteen and nineteen years old, taking turns carrying the tree on their shoulders. They stood it in the center of the compound. They made decorations from anything that glimmered,

as if they were children. Gum and candy wrappers were made into shimmering light reflectors; food package ribbons became frilly bows and streaming garland.

He looked at the tree. Sadness came over him. This was Christmas morning. No mass this year; no clergy. It was miles to the bases, on either side. Abandoned, dried-up rice paddies and defoliated stretches between them; a no-man's land. He walked into his bunker. He had less than three hours to eat and catch some shut-eye before their turn to man the perimeter. A note was on his table. They were sending a priest to them. He smiled. It is a day for miracles. He grabbed the note and ran out of the bunker. Sleep would come later.

He heard the thunder of choppers and a bugle blasting in the distance. He ran to the tower. The tower watchman yelled down that a half-track personnel carrier was coming straight toward them; a marine squad in the back; one of them blowing a bugle. They were escorted by two Cobra gunships flying above watching the tree line. The half-track entered the compound. The marine blowing the bugle was the priest.

The priest held the Christmas mass; the sermon: the miracle of Christ and the charge of forgiveness for mankind. The leader spoke to the priest after the mass and then walked across the compound. He went into the doped marine's bunker; the man still on the ground in a stupor. He grabbed the man's gear and piled it near the door. He tore open two c-ration packs and grabbed the packs of instant coffee from them and went over to the marine. He ripped open a coffee pack, opened the marine's mouth and dumped the coffee in. The leader waited. The

Fooling around posing for "gungy" picture to send home.

marine threw up, violently. When the marine's heaving stopped, the leader put the second pack into the marine's mouth. The marine gagged; his stomach convulsing. He rolled around on the ground in his own vomit. The leader sat on the marine's cot for a moment, then took the man's helmet and filled it with water. The marine looked up at him; sick but out of his stupor.

"Get cleaned up," the leader said, handing him the helmet full of water. "You're going back to command base with the priest. I told him you were sick. That's all the others need to know; nothing going on your record about this. Don't screw up again." The leader turned and left.

The gunships came to escort the priest back. The priest put the bugle to his lips and blew charge as they left the tower perimeter. He thought about the priest's charge with the bugle, and Christ's charge of forgiveness. The leader smiled and walked to his bunker. He wanted to write his Love; his miracle.

CHAPTER 24

We're Not Them

The chopper came in low and fast over the tree line in the early dawn light, setting down in the clearing. The marine sergeant's squad jumped from the rear ramp. Enemy fire erupted from all sides. The chopper's side gunners opened up with their fifty-caliber machine guns, their bullets ripping into the tree line, cutting down branches and small trees; trying to give the pilot a chance to lift off. Enemy bullets pierced through the chopper's shell; the pilot's window burst apart.

Iron Eagles picking marines up for a search-and-destroy mission in the valley

"Get the hell out of here," the sergeant yelled to the pilot. He moved his hand in a circular motion, his fingers extended; the lift-off signal. The squad made a defensive circle around the chopper, blasting the tree line to suppress the enemy fire long enough for the chopper to lift out.

"Guns up," the sergeant screamed to the M-60 machine-gun team. He pointed to muzzle flashes from around a big tree. "Rip 'em hard." The chopper lifted up, smoke coming from inside the cabin. It turned to the east, and then climbed up and over the treetops. The marines concentrated their fire on the rifle flashes coming from the jungle's edge. The enemy fire ceased.

"On me," the sergeant commanded. He moved toward the base of the mountain, concentrating on the terrain in front of them. His men fell in behind him, watching the tree lines on both sides. He moved them up the mountain.

They were part of a three-point assault team targeting a main VC base on the mountain; ARVNs coming from the west; a second marine unit north of the base as a block force. The sergeant broke trail for one click. He signaled up his point man. The man hesitated.

"Man, I don't wanna be there," he said. The sergeant knew him well. He came from the Bronx, grew up hard.

"Do what you fear or you'll regret it the rest of your life. You go three blocks, I'll go three blocks. We'll call it the double spear point. It'll be famous," the sergeant said.

"Man, VCs all over this mountain," the point man muttered in his Bronx accent.

"That's why we're here. We're going to their house. I need you at point."

"Yeah, right," he replied. He checked his clip, flashed a grin at the sergeant and headed up.

Firefights sounded around them all morning. The point men switched every few hundred yards; dense vegetation and nerves wore them down. They reached the southern point of the VC base late morning. No enemy to be seen.

Small-arms fire toward the north. The VC met the second marine force. The men stayed focused and worked their way, hut by hut, through the compound. Movement ahead; part of the ARVN force stood by huts next to the fire pit in the center of the compound as the marines swept in. The huts housed hospital beds. The sergeant saw that the ARVN force had captured four women. Nurses, he thought. A three-man guard team stayed to hold them.

He heard a scream. Three women were lying on the ground. They had been beaten. One of the ARVNs had his trousers down; his hand gripped the hair of the fourth nurse, forced on her knees in front of him. Her face was bloody, her arms hung at her side at odd angles. The ARVN punched her. The sergeant and point man ran over. The sergeant grabbed the ARVN's arm poised to strike her again.

"Leave 'em alone," he said. The ARVN faced him. The sergeant saw the officer patch on his collar.

"VC do to ours," the ARVN said in slang English.

"We're not them," the sergeant said. The woman looked up at him. She tried to speak. Her battered jaw could not work. Her eyes were void of emotion. Her soul had been emptied.

"You go next," the ARVN said, smiling. The sergeant could not stop the anger that rose in him. He swung his M-16 by the barrel; hard. It caught the ARVN on the side of his head. The ARVN slumped to the ground.

"Get 'em out of here!" he shouted to the corpsman, pointing at the captive nurses. The ARVN struggled to his feet.

"You, number ten," the ARVN screamed at the sergeant and started toward the woman again. The sergeant drove his fist into the man's face and tore his shirt off as he fell. The point man grabbed the sergeant from behind in a bear hug.

"You can't do this, he's an officer," he yelled. The sergeant shook him off and ripped at the ARVN's clothes.

"Low-life bastard doesn't deserve a uniform." He stripped the ARVN naked, turning out the man's trouser and shirt pockets, looking for an ID. Nothing. He bundled up the clothes and strode over to the fire and threw them in. He walked back to the man, still on the ground. Something wasn't right. An ARVN officer wouldn't be doing this, unless he wasn't ARVN; he was VC. He swung his rifle toward the other guards. "Watch 'em!" he ordered his team. "No ID."

"We not them," the other guard yelled. They both pulled out their papers. "We not them!" he repeated. The VC lying on the ground had blended into the ARVN assault undetected. Other ARVNs entered the area and spoke with the guards.

"We'll take him." The ARVN lieutenant in charge pointed to the VC; coldness in his voice.

"He's yours, lieutenant," the sergeant said. He saw in the officer's eyes that it did not bode well for the VC. The corpsman ran to the sergeant.

"The nurses aren't VC. Their medic told me they were taken from their vill months ago. We'll get 'em out on a medevac." he said.

"On me," the sergeant said to his team. The squad moved past the Vietnamese women. They were being cared for by the ARVNs. The marines swept north through the vill, toward the firefight. A gunshot rang out from behind them, just one, coming from the base center. The point man and the sergeant exchanged glances.

"Keep moving," the sergeant said to his point. "They do things different than us. We're not them."

CHAPTER 25

Show and Tell

The marine sergeant led 2nd Squad toward the narrow tree line. They were taking small-arms fire from VC.

"Lay down some cover fire," he ordered his M-60 weapons team. "1st fire team, stay with the guns, 2nd and 3rd fire teams; move up. "On me," he ordered. The two fire teams, three men each, moved forward, firing at the VC in the tree line. The M-60 machine guns fired into the enemy. Some VC dropped, others ran. The marines took the tree line. The sergeant signaled his squad to regroup, bringing up the weapons team and the 1st fire team. They swept through the trees. He counted a dozen VC lying on the ground. He heard rifle fire from the left flank, just ahead of them. 1st and 3rd Squad had moved to flank the enemy. The escaping VC made contact with 3rd Squad. The enemy was on the run.

The firefight started midmorning, four hours ago. The marines' search-and-destroy operation made contact with the VC force, driving them back to their old haunts on the river bank. The VC had food supplies and large amounts of ammo in underground caches.

The sergeant heard the rumbling of the behemoth behind him. It was an ARVN tank. He raised his hand with clenched fist, a signal for the tank men to hold back. It would not fire without the order. The ARVN tanks were on this operation with them. The sergeant was thinking about the ammo. A tank shell could set off an explosion. His men were too close to the caches.

The marine with squad leaders; the tanks in the back gave their mission support.

The ARVN tanks stopped just inside the tree line. Some of their tank crew got out and went to the dead VC. The sergeant saw them start to put them in clear body bags. Why the clear bags, he thought.

He led the 2nd Squad toward the river bank. There was only the river for the enemy to go to for escape. And now 2nd Squad covered that means, controlling the shore line. The VC had no place to go. They fought hard, some shooting from small holes made in the ground, some firing from trenches. A group started toward the river, two of them had RPGs. They turned to fire on the marines.

"Get the RPGs," the sergeant said pointing to them. His gun team downed one of them. He stopped the other. The marines' volley of firepower overwhelmed the VC running to the river. No one made the water.

1st and 3rd Squad had stopped the enemy that went to the flanks. The firefight was over, these VC done. None had surrendered. The sergeant regrouped the squads and formed a defensive perimeter around the site. The ARVNs recovered the bodies of the VC, and again put them into clear plastic bags, then piled them on their tanks. The ARVNs secured the ammo and food caches. The sergeant's radioman handed him the handset.

"Sergeant, the platoon will escort the tanks into the vill," the lieutenant ordered. "The ARVNs want the villagers to see the KIAs they got."

"What the hell for?"

"Propaganda."

The sergeant was speechless for a moment. He didn't want his men in a corpse parade.

"Lieutenant, if the villagers see marines with the bodies, it'll set pacification back a generation. The VC KIAs are somebody's family. I'd be more than pissed if somebody degraded my relative in a frigging parade."

"Get the men ready, sergeant, but hold there till I get back to you."

The sergeant leaned against an ARVN tank; VC bodies bloodying its dull steel shell, coloring it red: He waited; head bowed.

"Disregard that order, sergeant. We agreed with you, the captain knocked heads with HQ before they approved. But you will meet with us at 1000 hours tomorrow in his bunker," the lieutenant said. "The choppers are headed for you. You guys get a ride home." The sergeant assembled the squad leaders together.

"We're going back to the hill; the ARVNs will take a route through the vills. We're taking the high road."

CHAPTER 26

Instinct vs. Intel

The chopper flew through the pre-dawn light, skimming the jungle canopy. The grim faces of the men inside contrasted the serenity of the valley below. There were unspoken words as they glanced at each other. They were part of a three-team assault force being inserted into an armed enemy camp. Casualty stats: forty percent. Target value: high. Mission: destroy the enemy.

Being dropped in at mountain foothills for a search-and-clear operation.

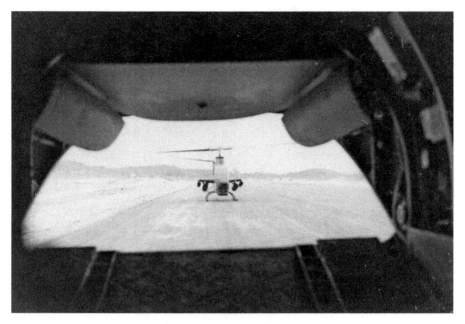

Gunships that supported the mission.

They watched their sergeant. His eyes focused on the cockpit. The signal came. Two minutes to the insertion point. He gave the command to lock and load. Each man took a standing position, their weapons ready to serve. He knew his men. They were the best. The casualty stats would be wrong this day. He looked at his men, checking their readiness, seeing their lips move in silent prayer.

He felt the rush of adrenalin as the chopper started down for the LZ. The side gunners opened fire with their fifty-caliber machine guns, spraying the zone to suppress any enemy fire. The clearing, a hundred yards from the vill, so small only one assault team could be inserted at a time. Two Cobra gunships circled to give supporting fire. Their chopper neared the ground. He gave the command and his team jumped. They landed in the jungle grass, and fired into the tree line, giving protective fire for the other two teams coming in.

The sergeant looked toward the vill. No return fire from the tree line or the vill. He could smell the smoke from the cook fires as it sifted through the air. He saw movement to his right. Someone ran between two straw huts carrying something close to their chest. The person stopped, laid the bundle gently on the ground and ran along the edge of the camp. The sergeant's senses registered all this in an instant. His rifle seemed to come to life in his hands, a well-honed instrument of peace or death. His finger started the trigger pull, his sight on the target.

His instincts felt something was wrong. Why would the person run to the side when it would be certain death, instead of back through the huts of the village? There still was no return fire. The feeling that he had would not let him finish the trigger pull. He raised his arm in a cease-fire gesture. His men stopped their cover fire. An intelligence officer embedded with his squad cursed him for not shooting the gook. He turned toward the officer, his M-16 still at the ready. Their eyes locked. His steel-cold stare silenced the officer.

He went to where the person had put down the bundle and used the barrel of his M-16 to move aside the cloth wrapping. An infant girl with big dark eyes full of fear looked back at him. She started to cry. Moving his rifle away, he put his fingers to his lips and shushed the child. She stopped crying and just looked at him. The person who put her down here had hoped to draw their fire away from their little girl. The radioman signaled for him. The chopper pilot was calling. Cradling the handset next to his ear, his eyes still vigilant for signs of the enemy, he heard why he felt something was wrong with this mission. He passed the handset to the intel officer. He watched the color drain from the officer's face. Intelligence had given him the wrong coordinates. They had been dropped into the wrong village. This village was friendly.

The war-weary villagers returned. The parent came and picked up the child. Before rushing away, they bowed their head in a gesture of thanks. The sergeant put a closed hand over his heart in acknowledgement. They both knew the divine had intervened. He gave the command to saddle up, feeling at peace. They all would be safe; this day.

CHAPTER 27

Leap of Faith

The trip flares burst in front of the marine compound, setting the darkness of the night on fire. One; then another; and another: bursting faster than the eye could follow. The images moved in a blur. Within seconds a hundred yards of flares ignited. The concertina wire could not hold them, the enemy too powerful to constrain. The marines on the bunkers opened fire. Three machine guns stationed along the bunker came alive, one after another laying out devastating fields of fire, covering the assault area with so tight a pattern a fly could not penetrate. The claymores were triggered, their blasts impervious to the enemy.

"I want daylight," the leader ordered the mortar crew. They could not see the enemy. When they thought they saw images, they were gone; setting the next rows of flares off, but always just a shadow, a motion; a ghost; just inside of the first row of wire. This was not a known enemy, something different. It was not moving toward them but moved across the front, never stopping its sideways thrust.

One hundred, two hundred yards the enemy ran through the darkness, the flares' light always cast where they had been, not where they were. The rushing noise of the mortar rounds leaving the tube added to the pulsing sound of rifle and machine-gun fire. The enemy still moved so fast the firepower of the marines could not catch up with it. Three hundred yards; it followed the concertina wire. The boom as the illumination rounds burst, marking their crescendo, slammed home the tempo of war, and gave out the brilliant light of day. The leader saw the enemy. His heart jumped.

"Cease fire, cease fire," he ordered. The enemy he saw: a tiger. It had entered the first wire then turned and was trapped in the wire's maze. The only way out was through, or over the concertina wire, an impossible leap. The only sound over the compound: the tiger's low growl. The marines on the perimeter watched the magnificent beast stop in the sudden silence. It looked toward the men. They were all quiet, standing now in awe. The beast's eyes burned yellow as it turned its massive head back and forth, looking for a way out.

The wire, three rows on the bottom, each as wide as a man is tall, two rows wide lay on top of them, all razor edged. The tiger's haunch showed dark red blood against its orange and black stripes, slashed by the wire. The tiger turned around, its powerful body just fitting between the rows of the deadly maze. It started to walk back and stopped. The leader thought it might try to go back out the way it had come. Freedom lay eighteen feet beyond this wire cage. The tiger looked up toward the top of the wire. It seemed to sit back. The muscles in its body knotted then released as it launched itself over the top of the wire, to freedom.

The silence broke as the men yelled in jubilation. The lasting image of the tiger landing clear of the wire and running toward the tree line made the leader smile. In this land of war carnage and death had been silenced, if only for a moment, by man and nature wanting the same thing; freedom for all.

CHAPTER 28

The Inner Enemy

The sergeant walked out of the command bunker after the briefing. The pre-dawn darkness offered no solace. Choppers would be here in an hour for their mission's lift-off. The platoon was to be inserted on the mountain. Part of a VC regiment had moved toward a friendly vill. A marine unit already on the mountain was headed to secure the vill. The sergeant's platoon mission directive: seek out, close with, and destroy the VC.

He walked toward his hooch deep in thought. The enemy was after food to stockpile before the monsoons started. He passed his platoon's hooches. Not everyone was there. They should be getting ready for the op. He turned and walked between two hooches, near the outside of the platoon's area. He saw a shadow of a man behind the hooch. The sergeant brought up his rifle. A man stepped out in front of him and blocked his way.

"Sarge, it's me," the man said. The darkness hid the man's face but the sergeant recognized the man's voice as one of the marines in his platoon. He lowered his rifle.

"What's going on? Where are the men?"

"A special meeting."

"What meeting?"

"The brothers are having a meeting."

"No time for that now." He started to move toward the meeting hooch.

"You don't wanna go down there," the other marine said.

"Step aside. Lift-off in less than an hour," the sergeant said.

"Be careful Sergeant. They're riled up tonight."

"So am I," the sergeant said and headed to the hooch.

He walked into the meeting hooch not saying a word. The men looked up at him. One scowled and moved to the back side of the hooch. The tension had their nerves coiled as if ready to spring.

"Good evening marines," the sergeant said. "We've got brother marines that need our help tonight. Check your rifles, ammo, water and eats. If you're angry, bring that with you. We'll put it to good use. In case you've forgotten, we're all marine green here. Choppers coming in thirty minutes; see you at the LZ." He turned and left.

Thirty minutes later the men were assembled at the helipad. He looked at them. He mentally checked off the gear he saw each man brought. Emotion and haste can cloud a person's thinking; the consequences deadly. All were ready. He felt pride in these men: the best at what they did. He heard the choppers coming up the valley; saw some of the men do the sign of the cross on themselves; others do just a subtle cross in the palm of their hand. The lead chopper touched down, the rear door opening. The sergeant crossed himself, slapped the point man on the helmet, the signal to load.

The three choppers lifted into the dawn sky. Their blades of thunder pounded their urgency; the echo resonated to the mountains ahead. The men on the chopper with the sergeant were silent. Not because of their mission. Some had been called out of their comfort zone in the hooch. The sergeant respected them; their diverse backgrounds; each carrying personal baggage from their life on the other side of the world.

He didn't know what inner enemy waited for each of them back in their hometown. But he knew the enemy that waited for them on the mountain. There was no place for black or white where they were headed; only life or death. He looked out the window port toward their destination; the mountain awakening to the tempo of war.

CHAPTER 29

Got Your Back

The seven-man squad braced themselves against the rotor wash from the three choppers landing. The double blades from each chopper's down draft peppered them with sand from the helipad. The rear door dropped down and the sergeant slapped his lead man's helmet, the signal to board. He looked down the hill and saw three more men coming, the last part of this special team. Late: he spit the dust from his mouth, more in disgust than the need to spit. He got on the chopper, and saw their scout sitting with his partner, next to the side gunner. "Gunny," he said in greeting as they shook hands.

"King, you remember the sergeant," the gunny said. The sergeant knelt down and shook hands with the scout's teammate, one hundred forty pounds of jungle-hard German Shepherd. The sergeant had been on another op with this scout team. The dog was sitting at rest, but leaned against the scout's leg, his muzzle on. He playfully pushed the sergeant with his head. An amazing animal the sergeant thought to himself, feeling a pang of sorrow. The dog's sixth tour; he would never be allowed back to stateside. He did his job too well; rumored to have fifty personal "confirms." He knew rumors were sometimes wrong; sometimes. King watched everything, sensing the energy and excitement of the marines. The chopper pilot looked back for the okay to lift the ramp.

"Three more coming," the sergeant said. The last three men boarded the chopper. King let out a deep growl and lunged at them. He came to the end of his leash held by the scout. His front legs slashed the air as he tried to reach them, hatred burning in his eyes as he fought against the muzzle. The three men were ARVNs, assigned to the sergeant's team for this op, against his advice. They bolted back out the ramp. They yelled in Vietnamese to the scout.

"What are they saying, gunny?" the sergeant asked.

"They don't want the dog."

"The dog stays. Get back in here," the sergeant ordered.

"Dog bad," they said and pointed to King, shaking their heads.

"Three men that get to mission lift-off late and won't follow orders, or a damn good marine who happens to be a dog; not a hard choice to make," the sergeant said. He signaled the pilot, his forefinger pointing up, spinning in a circle: lift-off. "Get on another bird," he yelled to the ARVNs.

The chopper lifted up, the door still closing. He saw the ARVNs stamping the ground, waving their rifles, yelling something he couldn't hear, couldn't understand if he did hear, and didn't care to hear anyway. He couldn't afford excuses; the skin of a lie, stuffed with a reason. He stood next to the scout and his dog; both now sitting relaxed, at ease, no sign of the demon dog.

"King didn't like those three," the scout said.

"We're better off without 'em," the sergeant replied. He realized there would be a discussion with the lieutenant later. Losing three riflemen wasn't a good start, but he sensed they would be trouble. The scout team was worth a dozen riflemen where they were going. He thought about the mission. A company-sized operation, their platoon's insertion point: the A Shau Valley, next to the Laotian border.

The choppers flew high to avoid enemy artillery, and then dropped into the valley fast. The marines jumped out before the choppers touched the ground, letting the big targets lift out before they could be fired upon. No enemy fire; the choppers thundered back up into the morning sky. The platoon moved toward the border. On the Laotian side, the NVA were building up strength for a big push on major targets, one being Da Nang. The marines' mission; break them up. The scout team led up the valley. The sergeant watched King. The dog's specialty was detecting booby traps and enemy. The scout had removed the leash and muzzle: King's signal to go to work. All communication to the dog was hand signals. The dog never stopped, running back and forth, checking out ahead of the platoon. They were at the end of the valley, and moved into the jungle.

The dog stayed closer, always looking back at the scout. The sergeant saw the dog stop and sit; the scout raised his hand overhead, fist closed. The sergeant stopped his men. They dropped down to one knee, facing opposite sides all along the column, rifles at the ready.

The sergeant moved up to the scout.

"He's sitting. It's a booby trap," the scout said and moved up to the dog. King had smelled out a claymore mine that the enemy set up with trip wires. The scout disarmed it.

They moved further into the jungle, the dense triple canopy cupping away the sunlight as if a giant hand had grabbed its rays and choked them off. They pushed in deeper. The sergeant felt thickness closing in. Not the vegetation; the eerie feeling that they were closer to the enemy than they thought. The dog stopped and crouched down. The scout dropped to the ground, the marines followed his lead; becoming part of the earth.

The enemy was coming toward them through the jungle. The dog had warned them in time. Small-arms fire erupted. The NVA had started their move. The enemy started to run toward them. The marines opened fire. Contact!

The scout team lay out ahead of them, with no cover.

"Guns up," the sergeant yelled to the machine-gun team. He pointed to his first fire-team, and then slapped the top of his helmet, the signal to move up with him. They needed to get the scout and the dog back. The machine guns laid out cover fire, holding the NVA at bay. The sergeant and the three riflemen crawled to the scout, firing into the enemy as they went. The scout shot into the enemy at his front. The dog lay with him, a low wolf growl coming from deep within. The sergeant didn't see the three NVA come from behind the fallen tree; King did. He launched himself into them. He ripped at one enemy's throat, the other two turned to shoot him. The sergeant and the scout both fired. The NVA fell to the ground. More came from the jungle slash. The marine fire team took them out. King was still tearing at the NVA he had on the ground. More came toward them. The sergeant pulled the pin and let a grenade fly; then pulled another, throwing the frag behind the fallen tree. Two more bodies fell back from the tree.

"King, here," the scout yelled to the dog. King did not respond, still attacking the enemy. The scout put his hands together and blew into them, making a loud whistle. The dog instantly came to him. They all crawled back to the squad. The firefight lasted into early evening. The platoon's fire superiority overcame the NVA, breaking their drive, for now. The noise of the firefight ahead of them became scattered as the NVA moved back further into Laos. The sergeant's orders were to move and join with the rest of the company.

He looked for the scout team to lead the platoon up. He saw the scout on his knees in front of his dog, arms wrapped around the big dog's head. The dog sat, leaning into him, with one paw over the scout's shoulder; a trusting bond shared. He waited for a moment then ordered the squad up. They passed where King fought the NVA. He heard the dog's menacing growl again and hesitated, looking into the jungle.

"It's okay," the scout said to him. "It's just a warning to number fifty-one," he said, pointing to the side.

The sergeant looked over and saw the body of the enemy that had fought with the dog. If it had not been for the dog, the marines' outcome would have been different. He thought back to his earlier decision to keep the dog. "Semper Fi, King, my friend," he whispered.

CHAPTER 30

Loyalty Rewarded

The rifleman ran into the sergeant's hooch. "Trouble," he said.

"What's up?" the sergeant said and jumped up from his cot.

"They won't serve the guys. The guy in charge says they need to clean up first. They're ready to fight."

Anger flashed in the sergeant's eyes. The marine platoon just returned to the command base from an extended operation in the valley. They made contact with the lead element of an NVA regiment. He looked toward the floor of the hooch at his own flak jacket; stained red with blood. The men did their work; work that he prayed no one else would ever have to do again. "Tell them to stand down and wait outside." The rifleman left.

The man in charge at the beer hooch had never been in a firefight, had never gone on an operation. He always had a bad foot or bad back. An excuse for anything that was hard. The sergeant grabbed a grenade, and started for the beer hooch. He rolled the grenade back and forth from one hand to the other as he walked. His anger and disgust grew. The men had fought hard and deserved a break. They watched as he passed them and walked into the hooch. The marines that sat at the tables grew silent.

"I hear that the men are too dirty to drink," he said to the NCO.

"They look like wild men," replied the man.

"We're all wild men," the sergeant said and when he pulled the pin from the grenade, the sound resonated throughout the silence of the hooch. He tossed the grenade behind the counter; the ping of the release handle as it flew through the air acted as a starter's pistol, everyone ran out the door, clearing the hooch. The sergeant walked to the door. "Come in and get your beer. You've earned them. They're free today," he said to his men who waited outside. He walked over and picked up the grenade. He took the firing pin from his pocket. He had screwed it out when he walked to the club. He screwed it back in, sliding the pin back in place. Walking back to his hooch, he wondered how long he would have to wait before word got to the CO.

Forty minutes later the order came to report to the captain's quarters. He put on his flak jacket, threw his towel around his neck, picked up his rifle and walked across the compound. He passed a group of marines standing outside the command bunker. He entered without trepidation. What is; is. His father would say, "you made your bed now lay in it." He stood at attention in front of his lieutenant and the captain.

"What the hell were you thinking," the captain yelled; the first words out of his mouth. The next few sentences were louder and just as unpleasant. The sergeant never flinched. He could hear the men outside talking about the captain's anger. He thought of the men, of what they came back from. They deserved better.

The sergeant respected the lieutenant and the captain. The captain was a Mustanger: he had come up through the racks of the enlisted men. Both good leaders and both seasoned in combat. The sergeant remained quiet and waited.

"Lieutenant, disperse the men away from my door," the captain ordered.

The lieutenant went to the door. "You men move on. There's nothing for you here."

The sergeant heard the muttering as the men moved away.

Anything you'd like to say about this, Lieutenant?" the captain asked.

"Just one thing; Wish I had been there to see it, sir."

"Me too," the captain said. He smiled then pointed to the coffee pot. "Don't pull a stunt like this again. Get yourself some coffee, Sergeant. I respect loyalty. The lieutenant is taking the platoon for three days of rest on the South China Sea; a place they call Stack Arms."

They talked about the past mission, its effect on the enemy and on the marines. They talked about war; they talked about home; and family. An hour later, the coffee pot empty, the sergeant stood. He saluted his officers then turned to the door.

"Semper Fi," the captain said and shook his hand. "Thanks for taking care of our marines."

CHAPTER 31

South China Sea—Three-Day Stand Down

The three marine choppers flew high over the beach in assault formation. The squad leader in the lead chopper saw the pilot hold up two fingers. Two minutes to insertion. They flew toward open water, then circled and headed back toward the buildings near the beach. They hovered, and then set down on the LZ pad. Chopper blades churned sand into the air, creating a crystal rainbow in the afternoon sun. The squad leader looked out the window opening. No enemy; no tracers.

The marines filed off. Their lieutenant waited for them.

"That, gentlemen, is the South China Sea," he pointed to the open water. "This is Stack Arms, your playground. Only three days, marines. Don't get stupid." He led them into a large building with a sign on top; MAG Sixteen. The officer of the day sat at the desk in front: rifle racks behind him; twenty or so already filled, the M-16s standing as if at attention. The squad leader wiped down his rifle, uneasy. He caught the officer of the day's glance.

"It'll be safe here. You have my word," the officer said. The squad leader wiped off the last of the sand dust and placed his rifle in the rack.

He went into a building marked NCO Quarters: a real bed with springs and a mattress three inches thick. He sat on the edge, laying his helmet and flak jacket on the floor. The first real bed he had been on in over five months. He let out a slow breath, his muscles relaxed. His mind allowed a calmness to enter.

He thought of his Love. She would be at work now. "It keeps my mind busy and away from the six o'clock news," she had told him. He missed her soft words and warm embrace, like when they sat in the car at the A & W drive-in diner and talked about their future children's names; and their house with a white picket fence.

He lay down on the bed, his arms around the pillow. He thought of her dark brown eyes that sparkled when she smiled. He longed for her touch, to hear her laugh. He ached for her, half a world away.

The marine's itinerary for the rest of the day and into the night: beer, burgers, and beach. At the picnic tables, he saw a few marines had had more than enough beer. Two draped over the tables; passed out. Men wrote catch-up letters in the lantern's light; others grouped together playing cards.

"Want to play a few hands?" the men asked.

"Maybe later when you've had a few more beers," he said. He grabbed a can of Schlitz from a metal trough that was half full of ice and beer next to the tables. He walked to the beach and sat at the water's edge.

The moon high; the South China Sea shimmered. The waves rolled in, spanking the firm body of the shoreline. They touched the soft skin of sand then retreated, a tease. The waves grew bolder, going deep onto the hungry shore. The sand absorbed the force, held it for a moment, savored its pleasure and then released it; a never ending crescendo.

His thoughts flashed to her: Their love deep; but not yet lovers. He swallowed the last of the Schlitz, the frustration of wanting her too much to bear. His fist closed around the can, crushing it. He started to throw it into the sea, instead, putting it against the back of his head as a pillow; he lay back on the sand, and stared at the moon. He pictured her looking down at him. Peace and warmth encompassed him, and lulled him to sleep.

The sound of running feet jarred him awake. He opened his eyes but didn't move. Instinct said wait. Someone grabbed his shoulders. He seized a hand and flipped a man over him. He grabbed a second man by the throat and kicked his legs out from under him. The man fell to his knees. In that instant he recognized them: Two marines in his squad.

"What the hell were you thinking," the squad leader yelled.

"We'd bet we could throw you in," the marine said. He rose, dripping from the surf. The squad leader heard laughter. He looked further back on the beach. More marines walked over.

"Pay up dude," one of them said to the man who had been on his knees. "We told them it was a stupid idea," he said to the squad leader and offered him a beer. He took it and sat down. The rest joined him.

He listened as they talked into the night; about missions; about their loved ones; about the future that waited for them back in the world; and they talked about Death lying in wait.

"Most not old enough to vote: but old enough to die," the squad leader said. He raised his beer high, the rest followed. "A salute to long life," he said. They fell quiet as the morning sun rose out of the sea, the promise of a new day; not the promise of peace.

The men headed back to their quarters. The squad leader walked up the beach. He thought back to his reaction to the marines' playful ambush. He trembled. Instinct and reaction honed to a razor's edge kept them alive in the Bush: but what happens when they go back to the world? Who would understand?

Most of the men slept until the sun was midway in the sky. The rest of the day: carefree; more beer. A marine went into the sea on an air mattress. A Cobra gunship flying back from a mission saw his struggle to get back to the shore: the man just a speck in the horizon.

The squad leader took four volunteers; a flat-bottomed row boat and went to get him. The boat would not stay on a straight course. The volunteers did not know how to row, two moving the paddles back and forth without lifting them from the water. He wasn't sure if it was inability or beer. He showed them, but finally, he rowed on one side, the other four on the opposite side.

They got to the man. He had a smile beneath his handlebar mustache. He was high on dope, his relief from the hell they were part of. Three of them grabbed him and pulled him into the boat. The squad leader saw his stash in a plastic bag tucked in his shorts. He grabbed it and threw it into the sea.

"You son of a bitch, I want that back," the man screamed.

"Go get it," the squad leader said. He grabbed the man's foot, and toppled him back into the sea. He started to row back towards the shore.

"You can't leave me here," the man yelled.

"A ride back or the dope; your choice," the squad leader said.

The man swam to the boat and grabbed the edge.

"You wouldn't want to ride with a son of a bitch," the squad leader said.

He took his oar and pressed it down on the man's hand.

"I'm sorry. Nobody is a son of a bitch," the man said. The men pulled him into the boat. They rowed back to shore in silence.

The lieutenant waited for them.

"You have any problems?" the lieutenant asked.

"Just discussions on life's choices," the squad leader said.

That night dinner was steak; two inches thick; sizzled slow; and individual baked potatoes; smothered in butter and sour cream.

Darkness came. The squad leader mingled with the men for a while then went to write his Love.

"Hey. I've got a reel-to-reel," the radioman said. The squad leader took the recorder and sat down on the picnic table. He talked to her on the tape; a little subdued because of the men around him; but also because the words came hard; his throat tight with emotion. He hoped it made sense. He took the tape and dropped it into the mail bag on the way back to his quarters.

He woke up in the early morning darkness: a commotion outside. He jumped up and went out. He looked toward the distant mountain and saw red tracers streak toward the ground: too far away to hear. Only a C-130 gunship had that kind of firepower. Rumor had it the plane could cover a football field with cannon fire every six inches in a matter of seconds: used to support ground troops engaged with a large enemy force. The marines were now silent. The squad leader watched the awesome spectacle; a mix of beauty and death. He knew where their next mission would be.

He thought of the marine they had pulled from the sea, trying to escape war's reality. "Lord, there is no rest, even here." he whispered.

The squad leader crossed himself and walked back toward his barracks. A cold breeze blew down from the mountains. He packed his gear. He sensed their rest time would be cut short; the aura of battle was in the wind.

CHAPTER 32

Tunnel or Tomb

The midday sun beat down on the twelve-man marine squad. They spread out to search the abandoned vill's hooches. A VC ran beyond a well in the center of the vill and disappeared. The squad leader signaled to his men and advanced until he saw a hole in the ground, the opening as large as a big hula-hoop. He crawled to it and put his rifle over the edge. Rifle fire erupted from the hole, blasting into the dirt around his rifle.

"Chieu hoi," the squad leader yelled, giving the VC a chance to surrender. No response. He fired his rifle down into the hole. Grabbing a grenade from his flak jacket pocket, he pulled the pin, threw it into the hole and rolled away. Dirt and debris blew out as if it was a volcano. He crawled back to the edge and peered over. It was an empty well, about ten feet deep. No enemy. He saw a tunnel opening near the bottom; an escape tunnel or just a place to hide.

"Got a tunnel, watch for the exit," he shouted. He jumped into the well and peered into the tunnel opening. The tunnel went in straight the length of a tall man then turned to the left. The main well for the village was fifty yards away in the same direction.

"Watch the big well. Looks like this goes over there," he shouted to a marine who watched from the top of the hole.

The VC had escaped into the tunnel before the grenade exploded. The squad leader did not know where the tunnel went or if the VC was still alive. The tunnel had to be checked out.

"God, please, no more tunnels," he whispered. He knew what awaited him; VC, darkness, and fear of being trapped underground. He would not ask anyone else to go in. He trembled as he looked into the entryway: only shoulder width; smaller than most. He took off a bandolier of ammo from his waist and held it in his hand. He wouldn't be able to get it after he was in. He slapped in a fresh clip, held his rifle in front of him and crawled in, pushing himself in further with his feet. His shoulders rubbed both sides. Darkness closed in around him; the outside sounds now hushed by the earth.

He pointed his rifle around the turn and fired three shots. The enemy's return fire pierced into the dirt at the corner. The splattered dirt stung the squad leader's face. The VC was alive. He heard the VC move. He didn't know if he was coming toward him or away. It heightened the fear in the squad leader. He waited. The sounds stopped. Fear pushed his heart wide. Blood pounded through his veins.

"Dear God, don't let me die down here," he prayed aloud. Fear constricted his throat. The prayer, his heartbeat, and stillness: the only noise. He had to go around the bend. He gulped in some air and started forward in the pitch blackness.

He screamed, and pushed with his feet, forcing himself forward and around the bend, firing into the darkness ahead of him until his rifle was empty. No return fire, just silence. He took out the empty clip and slammed a fresh one in. The smell of blood permeated the air. He didn't know if it was his or the VC's. All his being wanted to back out. The tunnel had gotten narrower. He tried to back up. He couldn't. His flak jacket bunched up and acted as a brake when he tried to move back. He couldn't bring his hands back to release the jacket. The tunnel held him tight; wedged in. He tried to turn his head. His helmet and face hit the wall. Dirt fell into his mouth. His teeth closed on grit. Fear grabbed at his mind.

He forced himself to think. He stretched his arms forward, drew his shoulders in and exhaled. He pushed with his toes and moved forward; inches at a time. He went two feet; six feet. The muscles in his calves burned. His shoulders dug into the sides of the tunnel. Ten yards: his mouth so dry from exertion and stale air his breath rasped. The tunnel started to get wider. It released its grip. He struggled forward a few yards at a time. He thought he heard something moving ahead of him but the tunnel was still dark. He pushed himself around another gradual bend and saw daylight: The end of the tunnel.

His breath caught. The VC lay between him and the end of the tunnel. He thumbed his rifle to full auto and fired a burst at the VC. No return fire. He wiggled forward. The VC didn't move; his body bloody. The squad leader poked him with his rifle. He saw the VC's rifle lying under him, backwards, barrel toward the squad leader; the only way he could shoot back. The ammo clip lay next to it; empty. The VC lay towards the light at the tunnel's end, hands clenched behind his head, face and elbows in the dirt. The squad leader did not know if the VC was alive and surrendering, or had given up to death, the tunnel his tomb.

He needed to move the VC ahead of him to get out. He put his rifle barrel into the VC's shirt collar and pushed. The barrel ripped through the shirt. He felt fear taking hold again. He put the rifle barrel under the VC's armpit and shoved him forward. He moved the VC to the edge of the tunnel.

"You guys out there?" he screamed, hoping the end of the tunnel was in the big well that his squad was watching.

"We're here," the marine said.

"We're coming out," the squad leader shouted. He pushed the VC's body out of the tunnel. It fell out of sight. The squad leader gasped for the fresh air. He looked down to see how far to the bottom of the well; six feet and dry. He tumbled out and fell on the VC's body, face to face. The VC's eyes opened and stared up at him; full of fear; then they closed. The squad leader picked him up and put him on his shoulder, holding the VC's hand up to the marine watching at the top.

"What are you doing?" the marine asked.

"Nobody's dying in this hole," the squad leader screamed. He couldn't leave him to die. That was between the VC and God.

The squad leader's body shook. It felt like the tunnel still held him. The adrenaline rush subsided. The marine pulled up the VC, and then reached back for the squad leader. He grabbed his hand and pulled. The squad leader looked up. The sunlight was bright behind the marine, the image of him blurred. He felt numb and weightless; floating in the air.

It was as if God had pulled him to safety. He fell on the ground away from the well and stared at the marine.

"Are you okay?" the marine asked.

"I'm not hit. Get him a corpsman," the squad leader said, and pointed to the VC.

The squad leader stood; his rifle lay on the ground. He could still feel the tightness of the tunnel squeezing the breath out of him. He ripped off his flak jacket and paced back and forth. He pounded his body with closed fists, breathing hard through his clenched teeth. He kept beating his body; harder; faster; until he couldn't feel the tunnel any more. No one said a word. They knew what a tunnel does to someone.

The squad leader put on his flak jacket and picked up his rifle and ammo. He walked over to the tunnel. The engineers would be there soon to blow it up. It would no longer exist, except in his mind.

Fear Will Find You

Enemy activity, high; heat, oppressive; mosquitoes, relentless; stress, like a bow string pulled to the release point.

The three-man marine point team watched the vill, undetected. Their mission: map it out; make no contact with the enemy. To their west, Laos; to their east, Nam: to the north, the DMZ. No lines in the jungle, just on his map; a triangle of death.

It would be dark soon; the vill too quiet for them to move. Dogs would hear them. The squad leader led toward the lower trail. They picked up their three support teams on the way. He set in a click east of the vill; claymores out. He looked toward his men, blended within the jungle.

His radioman started to fidget with the radio.

"Turn it off," he whispered to him.

"But what if we need it?" he muttered.

"If we need it, I'll tell you." The man's hand shook as he turned it off. The leader took out his canteen, had a drink, and handed it him.

"Pretend it's a boilermaker." The radioman took a drink.

"Cherry cool-aid? That crap will kill ya." He took another drink. "Sorry about the radio thing," he said and passed the canteen back.

The squad leader watched the trail. "Lord, get us back home. Thank you," he prayed. He was a "short-timer." Only thirty-eight days and a wake-up left in-country; then home on a freedom bird.

The night was quiet for hours. His muscles tensed when he heard branches break beyond them, toward the vill; too deep into the jungle to put eyes on. Something big moved, then silence. No enemy to be seen... Then there was. Silhouettes came out from the jungle to the trail; six enemy armed with AKs. He touched the radioman's arm, his eyes still on the enemy.

"Charlie's on the left; be ready." He heard the radioman roll over to signal the others. His left hand gripped the claymore trigger: his right, his M-16. Six would become one hundred six within minutes if it came to a firefight. "God help us," he whispered.

The NVA walked closer to them. They stopped in front of him; two rows of three; ten yards away. He could smell wood smoke on their clothes. The marines stayed motionless, invisible. One of the NVA leaned his weapon against his hip and lit up a reefer. They shared the smoke, passing it between them, talking soft. When it was gone, two of them pissed on the trail, laughing and then they all headed back toward the vill.

The squad leader turned to his radioman. The radio was there but the man was gone. He saw him a few yards away, lying at the base of a wide tree, curled up in a fetal position. Fear had found him.

CHAPTER 33

The Treasure

The sergeant gazed across the sandbagged perimeter wall. Beyond the emptiness of the cleared field of fire, children rummaged through the dump in search of anything their families could use or barter.

He had picked the dump back home growing up. But it wasn't to survive. It was for discarded toys that were still good or baby carriage

wheels for his homemade go-cart. He and his brothers would build them from scrap wood and iron pipe and coast them down the quarter-mile hill on the end of Main Street. One would watch for cars. The others ran, pushing the carts, then jumped in and zoomed down the road, the wind against their face, and their feet on the iron pipe that held the front wheels. Laughing, at times screaming, as they pulled the steering rope hard right for the sharp turn at the bottom of the hill.

Fun times: not like now. At their village at night, children went to their bed on the ground. Darkness brought terror to the villagers. VC came at night.

The sergeant gripped his rifle. Tonight his team would be outside the vill, waiting in the darkness for the enemy. The children would not know where the marines would be set in, only that they would be close; their protection from the night.

The shrill yell of a child finding treasure drew his focus. The child held it high: A wheel from a wheelbarrow. It didn't matter that the rest was missing. The kids gathered round, each spinning it as another held the ends of the worn-out axle. The sergeant pictured the children riding go-carts down a hill. "You are the true treasures," he whispered then looked around. The men might think he was losing it, talking to himself so much lately. He smiled. It seemed strange now. He didn't smile very often anymore. But there is something magical about a child making joyful sounds, even at a dump; in a land of war.

Vietnamese safe in their own home, at peace, that was why he was here. He headed back to his hooch to prepare the squad for the night action. He must not fail. There are treasures he must protect.

CHAPTER 34

The Torch is Passed

The rain beat down on the marines on the perimeter line. The sergeant watched the newbie trying to start a fire to heat a can of c-rations. Nothing would burn. The paper fire starter failed to stay lit. He went over to him and handed him a small piece of a white substance, the size of a thumbnail: like white fudge.

"Try this," he said. "Put it on the ground and put your lighter to it." The young marine did as instructed. The material immediately caught and flashed bright and hot. "Hold the can over it, but watch it. It's hotter than hell," he said. In a matter of seconds the can's contents were boiling. The newbie pulled it away, the can so hot he dropped it.

"What is that stuff?" he asked.

"C-4."

"Where do we get that?"

"You already have some. Hand me that claymore."

The newbie reached for the claymore mine that was near his feet, stored in a sandbagged cubby. The sergeant took out his Ka-Bar and pried at the back of the mine. "Watch and learn," he said. The back of the claymore snapped off and exposed the explosive charge. He slid the knife under the C-4 and lifted it out. He broke off a piece and tossed it to the newbie. The marine jumped back, eyes wide in fear.

He prayed the new marine learned fast. War doesn't give anyone much time; its lessons harsh and unforgiving. He remembered his first night in-country, the firefight he was in: And the firefight 1st Squad had a mile and half away that same night. 1st Squad never

Marines on day patrol before manning perimeter line at night.

came back. His squad leader's experience had kept him alive that first night.

"Look at me," his squad leader had told him as he grabbed him by the arm that next morning. "You did good last night. Watch and learn. Trust your training and most of all trust your instincts." he said as he held eye contact. He never forgot those words; or his squad leader.

He put the disabled claymore in his flak jacket pocket to dispose later. The C-4 he broke into eight pieces. He would give them out to the marines on the line. He looked over the compound. It seemed ages ago he was the newbie. He'd be leaving in a few weeks; still so much to teach them; so much for them to learn.

The sergeant shifted his poncho so that it still covered his rifle; mostly from habit. The rifle and his clothes were soaked even under the poncho. He headed up the perimeter line, making a mental note to have the newbie's squad leader keep him close. The lieutenant's briefing was in half an hour: search-and-destroy mission in the valley in the morning. They would be the first wave of the air assault. "God, please give them all time to learn," he prayed.

CHAPTER 35

The Good Letters Home

The marines' chopper thundered up the valley; an iron eagle flying back to its nest. Its blades cut through the pre-dawn darkness toward the mountain pass. It turned, and plunged down toward a clearing cut into the side of the mountain. Dust of Vietnam churned as it landed.

Iron Eagles bringing marines back to base after mission.

The sergeant led the twelve-man assault team off; their mission over. The pungent smell of gunpowder lingered on their bodies; boyish faces now drawn and expressionless. Their shoulders bowed under the weight of war.

The sergeant entered his hooch. An empty ammo box his table: a melted candle his light. He reached in his pocket and felt the loose grenade pin, not knowing why he had saved it. He took out his Zippo lighter, flipped it open, and spun the flint wheel. He stared at the flame; thoughts racing home. He yearned for her touch to renew his soul. The fire burned his fingers and brought his thoughts back. He lit the candle then snapped the Zippo's cover closed: the lighter's flame extinguished; but not the heat of his thoughts.

He lay on his cot, rolling the grenade pin back and forth over the dried blood on his chest. He would write his Love tonight. But only good letters home; not about lives taken or lost. His mind relived this last mission; the child in the vill the NVA had attacked. The boy, naked and bloody, ran from body to body, crying; in search of his mother. The sergeant had picked him up. He pulled him against his chest to shield him from the carnage. The child grabbed the crucifix that hung from the sergeant's neck.

"You can have that," the sergeant said. He lifted the crucifix's chain off over his helmet, brought the cross to his lips and then placed it around the child's neck. He handed the child to the corpsman and reached into his flak jacket pocket. He pulled out a grenade. "This is for those who hurt your mother," he whispered. "I promise."

The corpsman took the child to villagers coming back from hiding in the bush, hoping the boy's mother was with them.

The sergeant looked across the massacre. The brutality sickened him. Bodies lay in the doorway of their huts. The sixty yards of field between the huts and the jungle's edge were strewn with the defenseless casualties; women, children and old men. He walked over to the vill's central fire-pit and grabbed a handful of burned wood. It was cold. The cooking fire had never been lit. The vill had been hit before dawn; the villagers still asleep.

He dropped to his knees next to a woman's body, and laid his rifle down. His body shook. His lips moved in silent prayer. He dug his hands into the dirt. The earth wept red. He grabbed his rifle, touched the woman's hand and stood, waving his arm over his head in a circle; the signal to assemble.

The marines moved all night. They made contact with the enemy force as the sun rose. The first sound the enemy heard was the sergeant's grenade explode in their midst. The marines were focused, methodical, relentless. No enemy surrendered, none escaped; the marines' mission completed. And the promise kept.

The sergeant laid the grenade pin on the ammo box, and picked up his writing paper. He started his letter... "My love, sorry I haven't written sooner. We went to help a vill. A little kid was crying. I gave him my crucifix. We walked through the valley that night. I will never forget the sunrise..."

CHAPTER 36

The Flowers of War

The sergeant pulled out the map and checked his coordinates then directed the nine-man marine squad through the trees at the bottom of the ridge. He was anxious to get back to base; mail call today. The last two weeks there had been nothing for him. She wrote him every

The marine's Love; now his wife. They were married on January 23, 1971.

day but it took time for letters to catch up. He hoped there would be a letter, with pictures of her and the roses. She had written him about the red roses delivered to her that first month. She hadn't known they were coming: her favorite flower. He had set it up before he left for war. A dozen red roses every month to be delivered to her: for a year or his lifetime, whichever came first he had told the florist. He paid. The florist cried. His Love had sent him a picture of her with the roses, their blossoms as red as a sunrise on a hot August morning: his favorite picture. He would gaze at her with the roses and the war would become distant. This month's picture would be the last she would send him. He would be delivering the next dozen roses.

The squad came to the edge of a clearing. In front of them, the midday sun of Vietnam glared down on an open field, the steep base of the mountain ridge on one end, a bomb crater on the other. The sergeant stared at the tree line on the other side. Any movement would be enemy, his squad the only friendlies in this sector: A kill zone. No machine-gun team or medic with them today. He considered the options for crossing the open glade: all bad. The best bad option: one team at a time in the open. Fifty, maybe sixty yards to cross, like running from the batter's box to second base. He remembered the summers on his uncle's farm. He ran that distance around a makeshift diamond in a hayfield in eight seconds while his cousins cheered. These eight seconds would be run in silence; just the breathing of the squad behind him and the crushing beat of his own heart.

He separated the squad into its three-man fire-teams. "Anybody for rock, paper, scissors?" he asked. The squad knew he was joking to lighten the tension. He would lead the first three-man team across. The other two teams would follow on his signal. "Ok, let's go, box car room between us." he ordered. He waved his arm forward and then started their run across the opening. He scanned his eyes back and forth at the tree line as he ran, zig-zagging toward the woods. Sweat started down his face, his breathing forced through his mouth by the exertion. He burst into the forest edge and dove to the ground next to a moss-covered log. The rifleman and radioman leaped in behind him; their unsnapped flak jackets open as their chests heaved from the run. They expected enemy fire. The sergeant welcomed the silence. No enemy. He signaled the second team to cross, then the third team. A sigh of relief passed through his lips after they had all crossed.

He looked toward the top of the ridge, a main VC travel route. All seemed at peace, the quietness louder than the whispered secrets carried by the mountain breeze. A movement caught his focus. He knelt on one knee, raising his rifle. The squad dropped to the ground. The target stirred again, sixty feet up the ridge, about the length of three pick-up trucks. He saw the leaves of a mountain orchid wave as the wind waft through the trees. He moved closer. He had picked one on another mountain when he was new to war, a mountain bathed in napalm. That night a Vietnamese man died in his arms. He didn't know if the man was a fighter, or farmer. The man had been caught in the air strike. Badly burned, parts of his body dismembered, the napalm gel still burned on him. His last request to be buried with a picture he carried of a woman.

He didn't know if she was his wife, sister or friend, but he knew he loved her because he wanted to be buried with her. He had honored that request and then planted the orchid on his grave, praying for rebirth of both. That was months ago. He had never pulled another flower from this land of red earth. This was a different mountain: the same war.

This orchid's blossom was a deep pink, its core the color of white fire; like he imagined the color of passion. He knelt down, and cupped the petals in his calloused palm, the delicate blossom's innocence now cradled by the hand of war. He breathed in the scent of the orchid; his lips brushed its nectar; dewdrops of desire. His heart raced, his senses aroused; his thoughts now half a world away.

He glanced back at the squad. Each marine faced outward and watched for enemy. They had all taken ten-second war breaks before. Sometimes it's all there was to keep your sanity in this place of constant hell. They were granting him this private moment, his ten-second war break. He released the flower, picturing the day he would bring his Love the final dozen roses.

CHAPTER 37

The Longest Night

The beasts yielded their jungle to the man-animals. The nine men moved silent and swift; but methodical. The platoon sergeant led the marine assault squad across the base of Charlie Ridge: They were in the Kill Zone. They traveled light. No pack; no weapons team; no corpsman: just rifle, ammo, flak jacket, and helmet; their bush hat tucked into their belt and green towel hung around their neck. The radioman carried the com radio. The squad moved with a sense of urgency. They needed to reach their pause site. From there, they would wait until the fading light of dusk surrendered to total darkness. The sergeant's hand rose up with a clenched fist, the signal to stop. They would set in here for an hour, and then move to their ambush site. Two clicks east of them, a trail wound off the ridge into the valley; a VC resupply route. The squad's mission: stop any VC movement.

This was the sergeant's last night ambush; his last mission. Tomorrow night his tour was over and he would be heading home on a freedom bird. In standard procedure he would "come out of the bush" two weeks before his tour was over; most times. No missions or patrols. But the squad was short of men. They were exhausted. Replacements would come tomorrow, and then they could stand down for a couple of days.

The men settled to the ground to wait. The sergeant's thoughts were on the mission but he could not quell the anticipation of going home: He hungered for his Love's embrace.

"God, please have this be a quiet night," he whispered. He looked at his watch. It seemed time stood still. He glanced toward the squad.

They were hard to see. They had blended with the bush, the stone near the bottom of the trees, the mound of earth in the jungle grass. All had become one with the jungle; all good at what they did. Everyone a war brother, all put together by destiny.

Darkness had come. The radioman leaned toward him.

"Hey, Sergeant short-timer; is it time to go?" he asked.

"Get your lazy ass up and let's move out," the sergeant whispered. He hoped his thoughts had not shown.

Three hours had passed since they had moved to this target site and set in. A partial moon was midway of the sky. Good for the hunter; not for the prey. The sergeant looked at his watch; 0100 hours. His rifle brushed against his flak jacket pocket. He heard the rustle of paper; the letters. One, from her; the other his death letter. He started to smile. He promised himself he would burn the death letter when his freedom bird landed in Okinawa. The sound of running feet snapped his full focus back.

He thumbed his rifle's safety off, rolling into firing position, facing the noise. The squad all had moved into prone firing stance. They waited for the target to visualize.

"Dear God, not tonight," the sergeant whispered. He tightened his finger around the trigger. The men waited for him to open fire. Shrill sounds of squeals pierced the night; still no visual on the targets. Ten seconds: feet running; the sounds of bodies hitting the ground; hard. He strained to see the enemy. He looked to the rear, the flanks: nothing. He signaled his first fire-team leader to watch their backs and the three-man team turned toward their rear and repositioned to cover them. Thirty seconds. No target: just grunting.

"What the hell," the sergeant whispered. He rose to one knee. Wild pigs, fighting. A tremor went through his body. The adrenaline rush subsided. The pigs would not have stopped to fight if there was anyone moving down the trail behind them. "All clear, pigs fighting," he whispered to the radioman and the message passed to the others. He had the fire team facing the rear stay in position. The enemy may have heard the pig fight and moved off the trail to avoid the pigs giving their position away. They settled back down to watch, and wait.

It was two hours before daylight; the hardest hours. The need to sleep had an awesome power at this time. The sergeant took out a packet of instant coffee from his flak jacket pocket, ripped it open and poured it into his hand. He grimaced and lapped it into his mouth. His throat tightened as he swallowed the dry granules. His body jolted as the coffee absorbed into his system. A lesson born from necessity, sleep would have no power over him now. He focused on the trail. In three hours they would be back at the command base. "Lord, please get us all back," he prayed.

His eyes strained watching the trail, checking to their rear and flanks for movement. He held his breath when he thought he heard something, trying to gauge the direction the sound was coming from, only to realize it was nothing. Daylight was overpowering the night. It was time to head back.

"Saddle up, we're going home," he whispered to the men. He watched as they moved out. Jubilation filled his heart. His eyes moistened. This was the last time he would give that order. He really was going home.

CHAPTER 38

The Rings of War

The sergeant pushed the empty food tray away from him, grabbed his duffel bag and left the base chow hall. He stepped from the walkway headed for the tarmac. He was going home. He reached for his bush hat that he carried in his trouser leg pocket. It was gone. He ran back into the chow hall remembering he had left it on the table. It was not there. He asked all around him if they knew where it was. No one did. He sat for a minute, frustration and disbelief clouding his thoughts. Why would anyone take his bush hat? Then he pictured the grenade pins that were on the hat. His disbelief turned to anger; the only people in here were marines: marines don't steal; but it was gone. Reality hit him. People do strange things in war. He thought back to the night he put the last ring in the hat.

His knife glistened in the candlelight as he moved the blade. He separated the thin sections of metal that shaped a ring, then threaded the ring into the cloth band around the brim of his bush hat; the thirty-third ring: the last empty slot: The bush hat now encircled by the rings of war.

He didn't know why he had kept these grenade pin rings: he just had. He did not save very many. These all had special meaning; for different reasons. This last ring drew up deep emotions; emotions he kept locked down. Great sadness started tears; then anger, as he thought of their mission days earlier: VC had ravaged a friendly vill. His squad had pursued the enemy through the night; not the usual method of operation. They caught up with the enemy at dawn sleeping in a makeshift camp.

He had thrown the grenade into the midst of their encampment; setting off his squad's ambush. Throughout the hellish firefight, the grenade ring unknowingly encircled his finger. In the aftermath of the battle, as they secured the site, all enemy dead; no marine casualties, he felt the grenade ring still on his finger.

He had been called into an unofficial court of inquiry. He needed to justify why he had pursued the enemy through the night. He still sought that reason himself. Their mission directive was clear: to seek out, engage with, and destroy the enemy. That they had done. He knew that would justify his decision to move through the night. But in his own mind it was not clear to him if he had done it for the mission; or in anger: he had never killed in anger.

His captain had spoken up for him at the inquiry, telling the major that his squad had completed their mission directive and why in the hell was he being punished for doing that? He was cleared, and the war didn't flinch.

He looked again around the chow hall, getting up to leave, hoping to see the hat. All he saw was regular people taking a break, even if just a moment, from doing their work to help a war-torn land. New meaning sunk into him. The hat didn't matter to him anymore. He didn't need it to remember. And the marine who took it must be just borrowing it; he would give it back, someday.

CHAPTER 39

The Freedom Bird

F-4 Phantom jets, engines screaming as they powered across the runway, lifted up into the cloudless sky then streaked toward their target. Huge cargo planes being filled with supplies by men driving forklifts: at a hanger off by itself a plane being loaded with the bodies of the dead in black bags, carried by men who moved with the respect for life lost; a civilian airliner with men disembarking down the ramp, some dressed in khakis, and others in civvies. The sergeant sat on his sea bag on the tarmac of Da Nang Air Base, anxiety shaking his body. It was the same noise, same scenes as a year ago when he first came to Vietnam. The difference for him; he was going home.

He remembered that patrol through the vill a couple clicks from the base almost a year ago. He was a young lance corporal then, in-country a month. He was point man for the squad. They had stopped to take a break. An elderly Vietnamese man walked a few feet from them and on passing; he tipped his head in acknowledgment of the squad. "They are glad we're here," he said to his squad leader. The old man stopped and leaned on his hoe. Black pajama pants rolled up to his knees, bare feet, the few teeth he had left, black from chewing betel nut, no shirt to cover his hard, bone-thin body.

"We glad you here. You leave and VC come back. Same-same after French leave, VC come back. We here; fight alone when you go," he said.

"We won't go. America will never leave you," he had told the old man. The old man cradled the hoe in his elbow and stared into his eyes. His stare had searched his soul.

"You number one, but you will see; you go," the old man said. He watched him walk toward the rice paddies. He walked the walk of tiredness, not just age; the walk when hope is gone.

"He doesn't believe that we will fight with them as long as it takes," he said to his squad leader.

His squad leader put his helmet on, the words "Fu-k up the VC" printed in black marker on the camouflage cover on the back. He looked toward the paddy where the old man went. His face hardened. "He's seen so much shit for so long; he has pretty much accepted this life. We'll have to prove it to him," his squad leader had said. The day his squad leader went home he had asked him if he remembered the old man. "Keep proving it to him," he had said.

"Hey sergeant, you coming," the steward yelled from the top of the plane's boarding steps. The sergeant's focus snapped back to the tarmac. They were boarding the plane. America was still here. He was going home. He walked up the steps. His palm slid up the metal handrail, his sea bag slung on his shoulder instead of his M-16. It felt strange. He looked toward the mountains and Hai Vanh Pass. His mind soared beyond, to other places he'd had missions: Charlie Ridge, and the A Shau Valley, Khe Sanh, and the DMZ: Mike Tower, Arizona Territory, Dodge City, the Islands and Marble Mountain. He had never known the names of some of the valleys or rivers he'd crossed, and others, just their number: Hill Ten; Hill Fifty-five; Hill Forty-one. There were places no one would ever know they had been, somewhere in Laos and Cambodia. All these places he had sweated, and fought and bled. Others had died.

He boarded the plane; his freedom bird taking him back—to her. He crossed himself and said a solemn prayer for the marines. He hadn't had a chance to say his goodbyes to the men. He was with some of them on their mission last night; came back to base at daylight. Three hours later the choppers came; help needed in the mountains; an assault mission. They had planned to rest a while then have a last beer together with the lieutenant; say goodbyes. He had stood on the red dirt at the edge of the helipad as the marines ran for the iron eagles. Quick handclaps with some as they ran by; "Peep ya back in the World" with others. He had stood in silence as the marines embarked into their choppers. The lieutenant had looked back at him and stuck his arm out the window; two fingers in a "V" pointed up: Peace.

CHAPTER 40

Home

The marine stepped off the plane and followed the terminal signs to the baggage area to get his sea bag. Huge glass-covered advertisements lined the walls on both sides of the corridor; displays for eateries, spas, Seiko watches. He stopped in front of the Oldsmobile ad; the words "Escape from the ordinary" posted above the picture; a new 1970 Cutlass; matador red; embossed black letters on the side; 442. He stared at the picture, hands on the glass. "Someday," he whispered.

He entered the luggage area; stood next to the turnstile, and watched for his bag. The attendant, his father's age, came over; saw the marine's tour of duty ribbons and stood beside him. His sea bag came around and passed in front of them. The attendant reached out, pulled it off and handed it to the marine.

"Army: Normandy," he said. The marine looked at him, and then shook his hand.

"My father was Army; in France. You and he saved the world," he said. It brought tears to the older man's eyes. The marine saluted him and walked toward the bus terminal. He needed to get home.

His trip was delayed; late busses. He bought a coffee in the lobby café, and a paper dated October fourteenth; a day old. He drank his coffee and stepped outside. It was getting dark. Anxiety mounted inside him. He walked next to the building, staying in the shadows and stood at its edge. The city lights glimmered for miles. The smell of nutmeg and donuts drifted from the bakery across the street. Everything still open: traffic bustled: people walked and talked and laughed; at night; without fear. The closeness of this peace quieted him. He walked back to the terminal and got on the bus.

Ninety-six hours ago, he had been on a night ambush; half a world away; in a few hours he would be home; with her.

He sat midway up the aisle, seat tilted back. He took out the picture. It was worn and creased, being looked at so often; his favorite. She was holding a bouquet of a dozen red roses. Her eyes smiled at him; her dark hair fell onto her cloud-white blouse; her lilac skirt modestly above her knees but enough to stir him. He carried one of her letters with him, always. His thoughts hung on her words. Sleep found him; his dream: her.

He walked up her driveway. It had been over a year since he had seen her; or felt her touch. He reached the door and took a deep breath. Had he changed, he wondered. Who goes to war and not change?

He knocked, and the door was thrown open by her mother. She greeted him, pulled him into the home, held his face in her hands, and kissed his cheek.

"Thank God," she said.

"Welcome home," her father said and gripped his hand, hard. Her young brothers and sister all talked at once in their eagerness to greet him. He looked for her. Her mother caught his glance.

"She's nervous and ran upstairs," she said, with a nod toward the stairs. He went to the stairway, and up the steps, two at a time.

Maybe she didn't want to see him, he thought. Maybe he had changed too much. He reached the top of the stairs and walked into the sitting area. She ran out of her room toward him, releasing a small cry. He rushed to her; his arms encircled her waist; he brought her tight to him. He felt alive in her embrace; her soft lips on his. They held each other: The forever apart, now forever together. He was home.

CHAPTER 41

Innocence Compromised

The two marines sat in the bushes at the base of the mountain, back to back, few words whispered; watching the area around them for movement. Their mission: a two-man outpost to report enemy movements into the valley. The monsoon rain made visibility hard. They had turned down the volume of the field radio. Unless needed, the only communication would be a click on the handset every half hour to let command base know they were okay. Minutes turned into hours. Soon they would have to start to their extraction point.

The sixth sense that had been developed by experience told the team leader they were not alone any longer. He looked toward the mountain, breathing only through his mouth to intensify his hearing. He heard a cough. Feeling his teammate start to move, he grabbed his arm so he would not. He put his finger to his lips, signaling silence, and then keyed the handset to signal they had enemy movement, feeling the adrenalin surge through his teammate's arm. He knew it was his teammate's first op.

He saw the enemy, fifty yards away, moving down the trail from the mountains towards their position. Well-armed NVA regulars: he counted ten as they passed about thirty yards away. When they had passed out of sight, his teammate picked up the handset and was relaying the movement to the command base. The leader kept watch. Such a small group of regulars was uncommon. He prayed today would be different.

He looked toward the trail above them. His breath caught. More NVA were coming down from the ridge. The ten others were just their point element. He evaluated their position. He had picked this site to be able to watch the trail. There also was a natural ravine behind them. If they were discovered it would offer some cover. The NVA were now passing by the op team. He saw his teammate raise his arm, pointing back to the mountain; more enemy coming towards their position. He heard the fear in his teammate's voice whispering the numbers. He saw another group above them, coming down the ravine in back of them. The enemy was now on both sides of the op team, headed for the valley.

His teammate was no longer whispering into the handset; just staring at him, eyes wide; the fear in him seeing its chance to overcome. They both knew that any chance to retreat was gone. If they were spotted, they would die. He took the handset from his teammate's trembling hand and turned the volume off. A spurt of static now would get them killed. His teammate started shaking. He looked at him through the rain. He saw a man that was also still a boy. His teammate had his eighteenth birthday two days earlier. He thought back to his own eighteenth birthday. A year stuffed with a lifetime had passed since then.

He whispered to his teammate to keep his eyes on the ground so the enemy could not feel them; they would be okay. He put his arm around the man-boy's head, pulled him to his chest, and held him. His other hand leveled his M-16 toward the enemy; his finger curled around the cold, wet trigger that would spit death at its master's command. He had made his peace with God. He had accepted death, now it was just a matter of fighting hard until it came.

The NVA were passing in random force sizes. The leader's teammate had conquered his initial fear. Every time they had a chance between the passing groups, they prepared themselves. They assumed a prone firing position, facing opposite directions. Extra clips were laid out in front of them and grenades, with pins partially pulled, lay at their ready. The op team then watched and waited. If the fight came, it would be to the death.

The young couple lay in bed, feet touching, sharing the quiet comfort knowing their loved one was near even as they slept, the only noise the sound of their rhythmic breathing. The February moon shown through the window, casting its light on the calendar pinned onto the bedroom wall, highlighting the notation written in the third week, "thirty-day anniversary."

The man started to move as he slept, his arm encircled his bride. He pulled her head to his chest, awakening her. A smile flashed across her face, turning toward him, eagerly responding to his embrace. He whispered to her and the smile vanished, replaced by a questioning look.

"Shh, don't move," he whispered to her again, "They are all around us." She knew then he was having a nightmare, only this time she was in it.

"Who is all around us?" she asked. His answer sent a chill through her body.

"Enemy," he replied, his mind back in time.

His bride whispering his name awakened him. He now realized his arms encircled her, bringing her into his nightmare, a part of his past he never wanted her to know. His whole body shook, shedding the past to live the present.

CHAPTER 42

The Card

The man walked toward the huge brick building on the hill overlooking town. The imposing sign "Veterans Administration Hospital," chiseled in stone above the entryway, gave the building a stature of calming respect. It was intimidating inside. Long lines, waiting rooms full, standing room only. He had been coming here since his discharge from active duty months ago. Headaches that wouldn't stop, ringing ears that would not silence, skin that glowed like phosphorus under a purple light, discoloration that was getting worse instead of better. He had mentioned the flashbacks, telling them he locked them away in a secret room he had built in his mind. They would erase themselves over time.

He dreaded another day of standing in the same lines, well-meaning data-entry personnel asking the same questions: name, address, Social Security number, what branch served, and of course, how can we help you? He had answered these questions dozens of times, they had entered his answers in some ledger or data-entry machine, it was on all his records. The doctors had recognized his issues as service connected, but seemed to just kick them down to the next doctor's appointment. How many more lines must he stand in?

"How can I help you?" the lady at the desk asked. He looked at her, knowing his inner frustration was not her fault. She was not aware of how many times he had been here.

"I'm not sure," he replied. She looked him over, head to toe.

"Well, let's see. I'd guess about twenty, maybe twenty-one years old; quiet, with smiling eyes," she said to him. "Let's see how I did. Do you have your ID card?" His face felt warm. He handed it to her and she entered his number. She smiled as she read the info.

"I was right on," she said. She made a note in his file for the doctor and then she did something none of the others had done.

"Your records show service-connected injuries. From now on, this new ID card will also show it. You won't need to stand in these lines any longer. This should have been taken care of a long time ago," she said, and handed him the new ID card. He saluted her out of respect and again felt heat on his face.

"Thank you for being here," he murmured. He turned and headed to his appointment, wondering if today would be the day the headaches would stop.

The chair he sat in turned hard after an hour. They called his name; he went into the room. The nurse checked weight, height, and blood pressure, and tossed him a Johnnie.

"Clothes off; put this on, opening in the back. Climb up and sit on the table; the doctors will be right in," he said, and left. Thirty minutes later, the doctor came in. He looked tired. He had an assistant with him. She was younger and stood back a little as the doctor asked the questions. When the questions were done, the physical exam started. After the heart and lung check, they brought out the purple light. He stood barefoot on the cool floor. She turned off the overhead lights. They stood in front of him and took his Johnnie off: his face flushed; his skin glowed.

"Wow," the doctor said. "We'll give you a body lotion for that." A few more questions and they left. He put his boxers back on. The assistant came back in with the lotion.

He took the lotion, not unlike the other lotions they had given him to try. Frustration mounted within him. They were not sure how to cure the discoloring and blotches on his skin, just as they had not been able to stop the ringing in his ears, or his headaches. Maybe because it had been a different kind of war; using chemicals that had unknown side effects. It was becoming a learning curve that they were all on; the doctors, doing their best to find the cures: He, learning to deal with the war's aftermath. Neither were to blame.

He took a deep breath and let it out slowly, silently; relieving his tension and anxiety. It was a response he had learned on night ambushes to ease his nerves as he lay-in-wait for the enemy.

The doctor came back in.

"We are still working on lotions that will work best for you. You will need to make another appointment."

The doctor talked about the man's flashbacks and suggested an experimental program called bio-feedback. They would hook him up to wires and ask him questions about the battles. The man said no; he didn't want to remember; he wanted to forget.

The appointment ended. The doctor and his assistant left. The man picked up his lotion and walked out of the building. He headed back home; to the one person he thought about through all the battles, and now the memories: Her; his Love: Now his bride.

CHAPTER 43

Accountability Justified

The marines lay on the water-soaked ground; rain-drenched bodies like waterlogged tree trunks partially submerged in some backwoods fishing hole. Bush hats tight on their heads, weathered, issue green towels wrapped around their neck and faces, leaving only a small opening to see, protection from the hordes of mosquitoes. Time check: 0330 hrs. Their mission; stop the VC's attempts to resupply food and armaments. This was a kill zone.

The marine raised his starlight scope, checking the trail again. Rain had accumulated on the lens. He ran a corner of his towel over it, and turned the adjustment for better focus. He saw them. Twenty yards away; coming from the vill, headed toward the mountain. He touched the arm of his radioman, the warning passed to the others. He watched through the scope.

Seven figures; the three up front carrying large satchels slung from their shoulders, being prodded and poked by those behind them. Prisoners, forced to carry rice for the VC. They would be killed when they got to the camp. The location of the camp would stay secret. He whispered to his men that the first three were not targets. Triggering the claymores was no longer an option, not wanting the captives hurt.

The scope, water-soaked again, could not verify more VC behind the first group. The figures came closer. He waited. The trail passed in front of their position. Closer; closer; they were in front of them. He put pressure on the trigger: the captives were past them. He opened fire on the enemy, his first burst springing the ambush; his squad opened fire, giving them fire superiority. The enemy was overcome in a matter of seconds. The terrorized captives started running away from the trail, back to their vill.

One of the marines jumped to his feet. The leader yanked him to the ground as bursts of rifle fire sprayed across the trail. He popped an illumination round into the sky. Bursting into a brilliant light, it morphed the night into day, showing seven more of the enemy. A second element was behind the first, firing, not at them any longer, but at the captives. The marine's return fire dropped four of the VC. The other three started to run. One wore a bright yellow and red scarf, the other two covering his retreat. The darkness and the monsoon swallowed them, the illumination light sputtering out.

The marines swept the area. Eight enemy dead; the three captives, one elderly man and two girls, maybe twelve to fourteen years old, killed by the VC. The leader mentally processed his options. The old man was probably the village elder, the village's leading figure and that was why the VC wanted him dead. The girls were forced either because there were no longer any males left in the vill, or other despicable reasons. The old man should have been able to see grandchildren grow and the young girls should have been home brushing their hair and giggling. The VC who ran must have been high ranking to have the other two give cover fire. They had no conscience, no accountability for taking innocent lives. They would be back again to kill more of the villagers. The leader's face set like stone, his insides felt cold; as if he had stepped into a blizzard. He looked toward the trail the VC had run, and reached a decision.

He picked two riflemen to come with him, told his second in command to keep the site secure and to fire an illumination round after they left. It might make the VC who ran think they were all still at the firefight site. He turned to the trail, knowing the monsoon would slow the enemy down.

Animal predators that he had hunted back home got careless when chased, slowing down when they thought they were safe. These human predators would be no different. It would be daylight soon. Moving through the night's blackness, he was glad for its cloak of secrecy. Now, instead of cursing the pouring rain, he welcomed it, the raindrops pounding onto the ground covering the sound of his fire team.

Predators run toward a known safe place when chased. He calculated the VC would too. He pictured the map of their area of operation. Most of it was rice paddies or flat, open fields, with a few pagodas, until the foothills of the mountains. He remembered a swath of thick trees extending like a long, beckoning finger from the mountain foothills down into the paddies. The VC would take shelter there, the same way a predator back home would search out the closest cover. He picked up their pace, determined to reach the enemy before they could reach it.

The distance between them and the foothills closed. Within an hour daylight was upon them, the rain still constant. A hundred yards ahead loomed the tree line that the VC would want to reach so desperately. Somewhere between it and them were the VC. He signaled his team to a walk, searching for a glimpse of the VC, the magnitude of seeing them before being seen weighed heavily on him. He stopped his team, formed a back-to-back circle; giving them vision of everything around them. The rifleman pointed toward the tree line. The VC with the colored scarf was halfway to the trees, the other two close behind. One of them turned and yelled, pointing in their direction. The marines had already assumed a positive firing stance. Each knew their target. The rifleman on the leader's right would take out the VC on the right; the rifleman on his left would take out the VC on the left, leaving the scarfed VC for the leader.

The VC started firing wildly. Fear now controlled them. They had become the hunted, the prey. Death was closing in on them. The marine leader shouted "Chieu hoi," an offer for them to surrender. The two VC stopped firing. The scarfed one yelled at his men, then turned to run toward the woods. The other two commenced to fire at the marines again. The leader focused on his target, closing out the rest of the firefight. He slowed his breathing, his rifle sights following the target, his finger putting tension on the trigger. He felt the ground around him spitting mud from the enemy's fire. Part of his boot flew away from a hit, followed by a warm sticky flow. He remained unmoved, calm.

He knew what the VC would do when he gets to the very edge of the woods, his sanctuary of choice. All predators do it. The marine waited, heart beat slow and controlled. He exhaled, and increased the tension on the trigger. All predators stop for an instant before they leap to safety, to look back at the hunter; an animal to see where the hunter was, this man predator thinking he had escaped. The VC turned to see his hunters one last time. He shouted his contempt, fired his weapon in defiance. The marine finished the squeeze on the trigger, the rifle a part of him, answering his call. He felt the recoil; the statement final; his weapon completing its mission. The VC flipped in the air, landing on the ground motionless. Sanctuary denied: accountability assured.

He started toward the downed VC when he felt something strike him on the head, a sense of spiraling through a distant cosmic no-man's zone, with patchy fog so thick he found it hard to breathe;

He awoke realizing he had fallen out of bed, hitting his head on the floor; a nightmare from the past returned. He reached to turn on the light then thought better of it. This time his nightmare had not awakened his wife. He slipped out of the room. He saw his reflection in the hallway mirror, more than four decades older then the nineteen-year-old he had been when the nightmare was born. His face had a resigned look, wondering why he couldn't remember where he had left his reading glasses an hour ago, yet these memories came back.

He made a cup of hot chocolate, getting hot water from the faucet, not wanting the beep of the microwave to wake up his wife or daughter. The hot chocolate had a soothing effect on him. He sat down at the small circular wooden table, his thoughts returning to the dreams. He took a sip of his drink, feeling the warmth of the liquid in his mouth, savoring its rich sweet taste.

He slowly rubbed the table's smooth delicate finish. They had bought the table at the Christmas Tree Shop in Vermont, not thinking of its place of manufacture. His fingers traced out the words stamped into the edge of the table, "Made in Vietnam."

Acknowledgments

I could not have finished this work without support from my wife Barbara. I would write until late evening; lots of times not stopping until one or two o'clock in the morning; working to get the words to say what I felt. I tried not to disturb her when I came to bed; most times she awoke. "How you doing?" she would ask, or "you okay?" always supporting me. She was concerned at times that I was too deep into the memories; nightmares would come. Her quiet warning, "take a break for a while," she would say. She knew. There were times that my structure of words made a paragraph confusing and my attempts to capture what I wanted to say escaped me. I asked her to look at it. "What would you want it to say?" she would ask. Just by talking it out loud, the answer would come. At times I got frustrated with typing what I had written in longhand. She would stop what she was doing and come over to me. "Let me type that part." No questions: just quietly giving me a breather. She is my greatest blessing.

Our daughter, Jennifer, went with me to a reading of a chapter of my work; part of a New Hampshire Writers' Project event. She knew of my writing, but I had not yet shown her any of my work. I wasn't sure, during the early period, if I wanted her to know those memories or the nightmares. She sat in the audience as I read a memory about a Vietnamese child trapped in the horror of war. I saw her cry; my heart ripped; I thought I had hurt her. I told her after the reading I didn't mean to make her cry. She said she cried because she was a mother;

and it was war. She encouraged me to keep writing it. I thank her for her love and support.

When I realized I wanted to put the memories and nightmares into a book, I started attending the Writers Center of White River Junction. There, I met a group of writers who were serious about their own works and provided feedback to each other. I can't name all who were in the different workshops that I attended: I thank them all. There was a core group that developed around each other, of which I was blessed to be one. Strong friendships were developed. We seemed to meet at coffee shops; sometime planned, other times not knowing the other was going to be there and a conversation would soon follow about our projects. Joni Cole established the writing center and is the leader of the workshops that I attended. I thank her for her knowledge and her commitment and aspiration for us to thrive with our work. I thank Marjorie Sa'adah for her guidance; and passion for writing, that is an inspiration. Thank you to Mike Humphrey—who now writes in Heaven—and Dr. Donald Mahler, for their vital feedback; I thank Helmut Baer for his expert help with image formatting; I thank them for their friendship.

I appreciate, deeply, the vision of Casemate Publishers, who felt this manuscript encompassed a work that should be published.